# THAT ALL MAY BE ONE

HADDAM HOUSE is a publishing project in the field of religious literature for youth. Its special concern is the moral and religious questions and needs of young men and women. It gathers up and continues the interests that led to the publication of the Hazen Books on Religion and is directed primarily to students and employed young people.

Haddam House seeks as authors new voices qualified to give fresh guidance to thoughtful youth. In consultation with leaders of the United Student Christian Council and other groups, Haddam House is studying the changing needs for literature in its field and developing methods of wide distribution.

Policy and program for Haddam House are under the direction of an Editorial Board which represents common concerns of the Edward W. Hazen Foundation, Woman's Press, and Association Press, together with educators and religious leaders from various Christian churches and agencies. 

---

*Haddam House Books to Date*

BEYOND THIS DARKNESS, *Roger L. Shinn*
CHRISTIAN FAITH AND MY JOB, *Alexander Miller*
PRIMER FOR PROTESTANTS, *James Hastings Nichols*
PREFACE TO ETHICAL LIVING, *Robert E. Fitch*
THE GRAND INQUISITOR, *Fyodor Dostoevsky*
CHRISTIANITY AND COMMUNISM, *John C. Bennett*
YOUTH ASKS ABOUT RELIGION, *Jack Finegan*
YOUNG LAYMEN—YOUNG CHURCH, *John Oliver Nelson*
THE HUMAN VENTURE IN SEX, LOVE, AND MARRIAGE, *Peter A. Bertocci*
SCIENCE AND CHRISTIAN FAITH, *Edward LeRoy Long, Jr.*
A GOSPEL FOR THE SOCIAL AWAKENING, *Rauschenbusch*
THE CHRISTIAN IN POLITICS, *Jerry Voorhis*
REDISCOVERING THE BIBLE, *Bernhard W. Anderson*
LIFE'S MEANING, *Henry P. Van Dusen*
THAT ALL MAY BE ONE, *James Edward Lesslie Newbigin*

JAMES EDWARD LESSLIE NEWBIGIN

# That All May Be One

*A South India Diary – the Story of an Experiment in Christian Unity*

ASSOCIATION PRESS • NEW YORK 1952

# CONTENTS

# GLOSSARY

| | |
|---|---|
| *Catamaran* | A small boat made by tying together three curved logs of wood, the centre one being longer than the other two and serving as a keel. |
| *Kummi* | A chain of hills. A steep slope. |
| *Maidan* | A dance done by a group of dancers, usually women and girls. |
| *Panchayat* | A stretch of open ground. |
| *Pandal* | Originally a council of five. Constantly used for a body of people chosen to settle a disputed matter. |
| *Paraiyar* | A temporary structure of bamboo poles and plaited leaves of coconut palms. |
| *Pallar* | Two of the scheduled castes. |
| *Tank* | A shallow irrigation lake. |
| *Zemindar* | A large landowner. |

# PROLOGUE

EVERY part of the world is a mission field for the Christian Church. America is a mission field; within it there is the Church at work. Germany is a mission field; within it the Church is at work. Russia is a mission field; within it the Church is at work. India is a mission field; there, too, the Church lives and moves. This book is a narrative account of that Indian Church at work, as seen through the eyes of one of its ablest members. It is a record of the home mission task of the Indian Church.

Before one reads Bishop Newbigin's story, it might be helpful to reflect for a moment on the setting.

The author begins his account by telling of the overflowing crowd in St. George's Cathedral in Madras, India. He starts with the Church, but how did this cathedral in Madras happen to be there?

The city of Madras has meaning to the Christian in India. It was there, according to tradition, that St. Thomas, the Apostle, was martyred. Whether this is true or not it is historical fact that Christianity is at least fifteen centuries old in India. The missionary movement as we generally know it, however, did not begin until the sixteenth century, when Francis Xavier, companion and disciple of Ignatius Loyola, founder of the Jesuit Order, reached there and in the course of his work won several thousands to the Christian faith. Protestant missions began about two hundred and fifty years ago when Bartholomaus Ziegenbalg, a German, began his work, followed later by Schwartz, a German Lutheran, and William Carey, an Englishman. They did not come with much backing from their home churches; Church leaders considered their mission fantastic and unnecessary. The first American missionaries arrived in 1812. Since 1825 there has been a steady stream of missionaries.

The result is that there are now eight million Christians in twenty-five thousand centers of Christian worship. Much of the leadership is now in the hands of Indian Christians, but even today there are four thousand missionaries in two thousand different places of work. There are over three thousand Christian institutions including some seven hundred high schools, over six hundred hospitals and dispensaries, seventy leprosaria, one hundred and fifty orphanages, fifty-one colleges, and one hundred and twenty-eight agricultural co-operative societies.

Madras stands not only as a symbol of the Church in India, but as a symbol of a world missionary Church. It was there in 1938 that a world assembly was held to rethink and reaffirm the nature of the Christian world mission. Church leaders were there from every part of the world. The Christian message that had reached into India had during those hundred and fifty years penetrated into the most remote sections of the world. All the major continents were reached, and almost all the islands of the sea. In the years from

1920 to 1936, when the last world census was taken, the number of Christians in Africa totaled almost four million, a rise of 70 per cent; in Latin America, Protestant communicants numbered one and a half million, a rise of 90 per cent; in India a rise of 80 per cent; throughout the rest of Asia the average was over 60 per cent.

The Cathedral of St. George is in Madras for the same reason that the church in your home town is there, for the same reason that there are churches in every country in the world, save forbidden Afghanistan, Tibet, and Inner Mongolia. No other religious group is as widespread, as representative, as universal, as this Christian community of which the author of this book and we are a part. This has come about because there have been missionaries. There have been missionaries because men felt God had a purpose for them in the world. That purpose was to reach every man, woman, and child with the message and life of Jesus Christ. Lesslie Newbigin, the author, stands in this succession.

The past has made the Church in India a reality, but one does not have to read far into this book before realizing that the past and the present in India are not the same. To be sure there are comparisons, in fact, many. Age-old traditions, customs, ideas, persist, but there is also a New India as there is a New Asia. Anyone who reads the book and misses the nature of the change in Asia is like Rip Van Winkle who slept through the American Revolution.

What is the new?

First, there is the technological revolution which has engulfed the entire world but is seen in its most startling form in south and east Asia. The task of the Christian, unless the trend is checked, will become increasingly difficult, for within the revolution there are new forces at work.

There is, for example, the growing conviction that technological science holds the one key and the only ultimate solution to India's basic needs. The leaders of India as well as the rest of Asia are becoming, as are we, increasingly drunk with the possibilities of what technology can do to satisfy their physical appetites. In Calcutta, Singapore, Tokyo, as well as San Francisco and New York, the newspapers, the magazines, the radio, keep up a constant chatter that the satisfaction of one's physical needs is the real meaning of life. Man can live without ideas, without faith, but he must have Bread! The religious sensitivity of Hinduism with its asceticism has tended to check this trend more than in other parts of the world. However, even in India the childlike trust in a technological saviour spreads. It is now reaching the peasants, sifting through from the intellectuals, and the future will probably see this materialism increasingly at the center of their lives. This is a new factor in India with which the Christian must deal.

Second, the emotional atmosphere is different from the past. Whereas it was once placid, static, now one can feel again and again as he reads this book that trouble is brewing. The author tells of walking into the slums of a large Indian city. There, surrounded with evidences of poverty, he felt that the atmosphere was not as peaceful as it once had been, but rather that storm clouds were gathering, and there would be upheavals unless something was done to help these people. This feeling of uncertainty and impending change is characteristic of all Asia.

The religious massacres in 1947, when Pakistan and India were separated, gave some indication of the potential violence which lurks under the surface. But this has an even deeper basis. There is not only an awareness of religious differences, but another discovery: economic injustice. The simple people of India are at one with their Asiatic brothers, who toil and eke out a meager existence before life comes to an end in their late twenties or early thirties. They are discovering themselves. The people with whom the author talks are part of an old India and yet, as he writes, they are a part of a new India. For the first time they have seen that something must be done about their basic troubles. There is the fear of being left without a livelihood. In the past few years three hundred and fifty thousand textile workers in India alone have put six million home spinning wheels out of action. There is a consciousness that high infant mortality and premature death are unnecessary. There is fear of too many mouths to feed. In India the population grows by five million a year. Here India is a part of a wider problem, for there are in Asia thirty thousand new mouths to feed every morning. In most cases Christians in these areas are a part of this fear—they are poor, undernourished, living in mud houses, and dying before it is necessary.

As you read this book you cannot fail to be aware of the discontent of the people who surround the writer. They are restless and uncertain. Few of them understand why, but the feeling grows that there must be change or they will be pulled further into the poverty and frustration that surrounds them.

As if this were not enough, there is added the problem of racial resentment. This bitterness toward the white man in India is apparently mild at present, but all through Asia it is potential and in many areas actual. The white man represents racial snobbery, imperialism, and exploitation.

This new situation in India and Asia, which we are tempted to underestimate, has already brought about a radical change. Newbigin himself is an illustration. He no longer finds much help in the fact that he is from the West. Whereas missionaries before him gained prestige and influence because they were westerners, this attitude is fast disappearing. Simply being a westerner no longer cuts much ice! The reasons are not hard to find. The so-called Christian West sends out movies of a moral tone which is in many cases far below the moral standards of the non-Christians whom Newbigin would serve.

The so-called powerful West suffered devastating depression during a period of peace. Its apparent strength was an illusion.

The so-called democratic West saw Fascism come to Germany, race riots in the United States, and colonialism still a policy of Britain and France.

The so-called altruistic West dropped the first atomic bomb on a city filled with people.

The result has been that the West has lost its hold on the minds of Asiatics. To be sure there is still awe and respect, but nothing compared with the feeling which existed in the past. In Asia the West is on the retreat. The withdrawal of England from India and Burma, and of the Netherlands from Indonesia, is only a reflection of this fact. Coupled with this recession is the rise of other groups of powers—Russia and China, the Moslem League, and others.

As the West has lost its initiative, the Orient is regaining hers. She is regaining her pride in her race and colour. The Indian is proud of his skin and his cultural history. The Chinese is glad he is Chinese. Both the Indian and the Chinese want to participate in the use of power, and, what is more, they have the wherewithal to do it. Asia has become the balance wheel between Russia and the West. It is there that the great masses of men and women live, and as they eventually go, so will go the power balances in the world. The white man's day of dominance has ended. There is a new situation today, and the author of this book as he walks through the villages and cities is living in such a new India within a new Asia.

He shows us the Christians in South India not only living in a new and revolutionary Asia, but also facing more aggressive adversaries.

What are these adversaries?

The author writes of witnessing two parades. One was a milling crowd slowly making its way behind a massive idol borne on the shoulders of devotees. This is Hinduism. The second parade was a solid mass of humanity, locked arm in arm, four abreast, shouting and singing as they marched. This is Communism.

Hinduism is one of the two problems confronting the Church of South India. In other parts of the world it might be Islam, as in the Near East or Indonesia, or political Catholicism, as in the Philippines or Latin America, or Buddhism, as in Siam or Ceylon. But in India it is Hinduism. Hinduism strikes at Newbigin and his Christian flock in two ways:

The first is the attempt to swallow and digest them. This attempt to absorb Christianity is an instance of what we call syncretism. The Hindu says that Jesus is indeed a manifestation of God, and he is willing to place Jesus with the many other idols that share the temple. Hindus call upon Christianity to bring its faith into the ocean of Hinduism and, like a drop of water returning to the sea, to lose itself. When one remembers that there are more Hindus in India than there are Protestant Christians in all the world, one catches some glimpse of the power of this threat.

The second way that Hinduism strikes is through economic and political pressure. The economic pressure comes when Christians are refused work; in a land where unemployment means starvation, this can be used as a potent weapon. The political pressure is more a potential danger than an actual threat. The new constitution promises religious freedom, but Christians fear that some day a turn might come and the ever growing nationalism of India might be linked up with Hinduism. If this were to take place, to be a Christian would be interpreted as being unpatriotic and disloyal to the country. This prospect is a constant shadow over the Christian community, and under it the Christian Church works and lives. In Pakistan the danger is political Islam, in the Philippines political Catholicism, and so it goes.

Communism is the second problem. The Communists in India have not been very successful, and their violent methods have caused revulsion among a people who could understand and love a pacifist like Ghandi. But there is corruption in the government that eats like a cancer at its life, and the Communist ideas and organization wait until a more fitting hour when the soil is ready for action. As the author mentions on more than one occasion, the Communists appeal particularly to students and the dispossessed. These two groups are uncertain and discontented. The Communists call upon them to revolt. Both the students and the dispossessed lean toward materialism. Communism claims that materialism is the one reality and that technological science is the only real saviour. The students in particular are sensitive about race and feel deep resentment against the white man's sense of superiority. The Communists call for racial equality. With Communism promising everything and anything, the Church finds a real adversary.

Through this book then we discover the Church in a new India and facing many adversaries, but also having a new situation within itself. This is particularly true in South India. This is to be seen in the trend which we call "ecumenical." Lesslie Newbigin is Bishop in Madhurai and Ramnad, a part of the Church of South India. This is an example of what an "ecumenical" church can be. Although it took twenty-eight years of patient preparation, on September 27, 1947, one million Christians, formerly Anglicans, Methodists, Presbyterians, and Congregationalists, were united. It is this inauguration of which the author speaks at the beginning of his book. This was the first time that Episcopal and non-Episcopal Churches had come together into one organization, and all who were present at the inauguration ceremonies in Madras knew that they were at one of the turning points in Christian history.

The Church of South India covers an area rather greater than that of prewar Germany, extending some seven hundred and fifty miles up the Indian peninsula and including a part of Ceylon. There are fourteen dioceses, approximately half of them under Indian bishops. During the three years that have elapsed, the new Church has grown together. If one were to attend its general meetings today, it would be almost impossible to tell the previous Church affiliation of any speaker. This feeling of being one fellowship has given the members new courage in witnessing to the non-Christians. Finding unity, the Church has found at a deeper level its mission to evangelize India.

It is a steward of God's word. The message of His mighty acts, culminating in the life, the death, the resurrection of His Son, Jesus Christ, must be preached. It preaches to all men, but in particular it reaches out to the outcastes, the dispossessed, the poor.

Here is where Newbigin begins. He spends much of his time with the poor, for his task is to identify himself with them. This task is not easy, and he must walk a very narrow line. His mission is to be one with these who are struggling out of poverty, injustice, and filth. Newbigin is a man of great ability; he was a delegate to the Assembly of the World Council of Churches in 1948; he is the author of several important books; he has recently been selected to serve as chairman of one of the major commissions of the World Council of Churches. But these facts about him are secondary. He considers his primary task so to identify himself with those in trouble that they might feel that he is one of them, sympathetic with their needs, and determined to help them. When the poor find their wells dry, he tries to help them get water. When a farmer is hurt, he goes to serve him. When a mother is deserted, he is there to find ways of support. He writes, "Surely it is of immense significance that the Church has become rooted here and among the lowest strata in society."

Here is an insight into the nature of the world mission of the Christian Church today. It must become increasingly identified with the manual workers, the peasants, the underprivileged, with anyone who is cast aside. It calls for simplicity of life, consecration of spirit, and a conviction that identification with human suffering and need is the crucial area at which the Christian Church should direct its strength.

Although Newbigin identifies himself with the poor,

he does not fall prey to the belief that man's ultimate problems are physical. He sees, as all Christians do, that their ultimate problem does not lie where it appears superficially to be. It is this same thing that D. T. Niles is pressing home in the other Student Volunteer Movement Quadrennial book, *That They May Have Life*. Newbigin is reminding those whom he would serve that their fundamental problem is sin and death. He sees and illustrates in the book again and again the dynamic character of sin, its capacity to break up a family, to disrupt the Church, to cause exploitation, suffering, and premature death. It is to these two problems of sin and death that the author comes preaching a message of deliverance through Jesus Christ. He does not apologize for the fact that the proclamation of the gospel is at the center of the Church's mission.

But the Church is more than this:

It is a fellowship. The temptation in India, as the author suggests, is for some Indian Christians to transfer their cultural ideas of caste into the Church fellowship itself. But the Church of South India, as seen through the eyes of its leading Christians, cannot be limited to any nation, any race, any caste.

It is a leaven. The reader will quickly notice that the Church of South India is a democratic Church. If democracy is ever to have foundations in India, it will find a source of strength here.

It is a servant. It cares for those suffering from hunger; it opens schools on agriculture, medicine, science; it operates co-operatives for farmers and leather workers; it cares for orphans, lepers, beggars.

It is a missionary. The Church of South India has not only its home missions but it has also sent an Indian missionary family to Papua, New Guinea. It has a foreign mission outreach as well. The Church's mission is always twofold: intensive, reaching to every corner within the areas where it lives; and extensive, reaching out to the furthest areas that it has the strength to reach.

The Christian Church in India is a small, almost insignificant minority, living in the midst of a dominant Hindu majority and in a sociological and political situation fraught with many dangers. Although it is numerically weak and it is plagued with the problems of discipline and loyalty within, yet there is vitality and movement.

It may be that out of South India or some other part of Asia may come a Church that will be the center of Christian missionary activity all through Asia. Perhaps fifty to a hundred years from now it will send its missionaries throughout the world, being faithful as all Christians should be to the command to proclaim the gospel to all nations.

Although the book at first seems to tell of a pattern of life vastly different from our own, we soon discover that it does speak to our situation. The author is writing not only of India. He is writing about our own country where so many of these same problems are before us. To be sure we face some particular difficulties not experienced by Indians. They face some we have only read about. However, the underlying structure is the same. It is the story of men and women, simple men and women, some heroic, some cowards, living in this turbulent and swiftly changing period in history.

It is the Christian witness of an individual; at the same time it is the Christian witness of a Church, a Church made up of people of varied ecclesiastical backgrounds who in their new-found unity have developed a deeper missionary concern. It is the story of the witness of an Englishman hard at work in the heart of India. At the same time it is representative of the Christian witness anywhere in the world.

The problems are similar. There is fear of war, fear of sickness, fear of failure, fear of Communism, fear of God's inability to handle the situation.

The Church is similar. It is made up of frail creatures who are one moment noble and the next small and selfish, who at times succumb to the temptations of the flesh but at other moments will witness sacrificially to their Lord.

The Christian responsibility is similar. Bishop Newbigin's patience, his concern for the needy, his simplicity, his consecration, his faith in Christ's Kingdom as man's hope, cannot help but inspire.

For these reasons we have chosen this book which records a Christian witness in world revolution.

E. H. Johnson, *General Secretary*
The Student Volunteer Movement for
Christian Missions, Inc.

New York, 1951

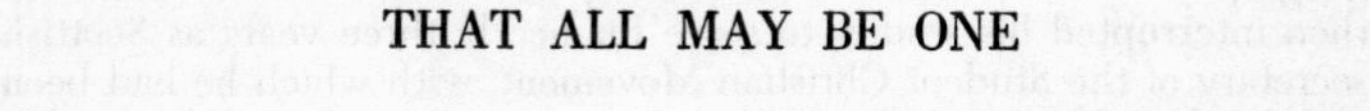

# THAT ALL MAY BE ONE

# ABOUT THE AUTHOR

James Edward Lesslie Newbigin was born in Newcastle-upon-Tyne, England. From the Leighton Park School he went to Queens College, Cambridge, where he studied from 1928 to 1931, taking his Tripos in geography and economics and making a distinguished record. He then interrupted his studies to serve for nearly three years as Scottish secretary of the Student Christian Movement, with which he had been closely identified during his college days. His ability both as a speaker and musician soon made him one of the most successful secretaries. After three more years in Cambridge where he studied theology in Westminster College he went to India in 1936 as a missionary under the Church of Scotland.

He was stationed at Chingleput, then at Conjeeveran, a great center of Hinduism in which he was able to see and take part in many phases of mission work. Contact was soon renewed with the S.C.M. and he became a well-known speaker at its meetings and conferences. Soon, too, he was taking his part in the work of the Joint Committee on Church Union. There his zeal for the cause of union and his firm grasp of the issues involved brought him into prominence. In the Madras Church Council his clear and thorough explanations of union problems and plans and his sincere and patient tackling of objections did much to lead the council to accept the scheme.

The gift of seeing something that is urgently necessary, the initiative to start work on it, the enthusiasm to arouse others, and the fighting spirit to see things through—these are qualities which he possesses in good measure.

He is a believer in evangelism—going out to meet men in the streets, the army, the monastery, the fields, or wherever they are, and facing them with Christ. He has a keen interest in the rural church with its problems of lay leadership, church buildings, and the like.

# ONE

At seven o'clock in the morning everything is still fresh and cool after last night's rain, and the cathedral looks its best in its setting of wide lawns and leafy trees. There is still an hour before the service is due to begin, but the cathedral and the vast *pandal* alongside it are already beginning to fill up. People from all over South India are arriving in a constant stream, and here and there one recognizes one of the delegates from Churches in other parts of the world. The inevitable photographers are everywhere laying their ambushes.

The last five days of retreat and conference have been a wonderful preparation for this great day. In three days of silence we have had a blessed opportunity for steadying will and desire and directing them towards God alone. Then in the last two days we have been able to take counsel together about the multitudinous problems which will face us when we scatter on Monday to our fourteen dioceses. One has begun to realize what a vast difference there is between a Scheme of Union, however detailed, and a united Church. It has been a constantly increasing joy to find that on all essentials we are already so much at one that matters of detail can be settled without any anxiety or friction. More and more messages have poured in from all parts of the world, assuring us that the prayers of countless Christian people are with us. Now the hour is about to strike for the great adventure in obedience.

As the cathedral bell strikes eight, the service of inauguration opens and the long procession representing the three uniting Churches moves up the centre aisle of the cathedral. We join in prayer and then listen to the reading of the great High Priestly prayer in the power of which alone all these long years of wrestling with our divisions have been possible. Then on our knees we confess afresh that our unity, holiness, truth, are in Him alone and not in us. One by one the authorized representatives of the three Churches come to the chancel steps and read out the resolutions of their governing bodies accepting the Union, and then go to the Holy Table and lay thereon signed copies of the Scheme of Union, and the signatures of all the ministers assenting to it. As each one does so he kneels before the Table and he and we together offer up silently to God a life given up that it may be won.

Now the three volumes lie side by side on the Table. There lie our separate selves. We have been proud of them, these great names, great principles, secure traditions of faith and worship, beloved patterns of holiness. We shall sometimes look back, because the flesh is weak. But 'pearls for pearls' is the law of God's Kingdom. Lord, receive these goodly pearls which Thou prayers of Thy people and blessed the labours of Thy gavest! We are praying again: 'Thou hast heard the servants, and hast brought us to this day for the glory of Thy name. In obedience to Thy will and led by Thy Spirit, as we accept one another as fellow members and fellow ministers, do Thou strengthen the bonds between us and unite us and make us one body, Thyself, O Christ, being its Head. Make us all of one heart and of one soul, united in one holy bond of truth and peace, of faith and charity.' Now we are on our feet and the Bishop's voice is ringing through the cathedral. 'By authority of the governing bodies whose resolutions have been read in your hearing . . . I declare that these three Churches . . . are now become one Church of South India.' A great peal from the organ breaks in upon the words and in a moment four thousand voices burst into the *Te Deum* in one tremendous shout of praise. All the long-frustrated desires of these last painful years have burst through the dam and are flowing in one irresistible flood. We look at each other with a kind of wonder; we are no longer friendly strangers but brothers in one household. With God all things are possible. Is this a dream or is this really true? Surely the heavenly choir is joining with us as we sing, and all those good men of faith who went before us not having received the promises but having seen them and greeted them from afar. 'To Thee Cherubim and Seraphim continually do cry Holy, Holy, Holy.' We are brought down to earth by discovering that something has gone wrong with the singing. The printer has skipped 'the goodly fellowship of the prophets,' and there is a temporary breach of unity between those who follow the book and those who sing from memory. It is fitting that we remember that we are earthen vessels. 'O Lord, have mercy upon us, have mercy upon us. O Lord, let thy mercy lighten upon us as our trust is in thee. O Lord, in thee have I trusted, let me never be confounded.'

We are seated again and ready for the second part of the service, that which concerns 'the unification of the ministry.' Bishops and other ministers whose authority has hitherto extended only to the bounds of the separate Churches are commissioned with prayer to exercise that ministry throughout the wider fellowship that is now ours. We sing a hymn that lifts our hearts and minds up to the ascended and regnant Christ, who having led captivity captive gave gifts unto men. And then out into the bright morning sunshine for a brief interval before the second service.

What has been done? Not, if we speak strictly, the inauguration of a 'Church.' There can be but one Church. What has been done is that something which hid the true character of the Church has been repented of, and a very small step has been taken towards putting it away. Even that little step could not have been taken without the tremendous and ceaseless constraint of God's Word and Spirit. Now there is a sense of joy and release. God save us from settling down again.

Fifteen minutes later we are slowly moving up the aisle of the cathedral for the second service of the day. Nine presbyters of the Church of South India are to be made bishops. As the service moves on it is borne in on one that here the truly Catholic and the truly Evangelical are one, that at the heart of true worship these things do not need to be patched together but are found to belong together. As we kneel at the rail the figure of Christ rising from the tomb faces us to meet the sickening sense of utter unfitness for so great a task. Then our first communion together, about 3,500 communicants taking part, a true foretaste of the heavenly banquet and a season of joy that none of us will forget.

## TWO

THE glow of union is still upon us! On Saturday night there was a great open-air meeting and it seemed as if no one wanted to go home after it was over, so eager was everyone to talk about the great event of the day. On Sunday there were special thanksgivings in all the churches, and everywhere kindness and thankfulness —surely the work of God's Spirit. Now we are all leaving Madras for our various dioceses, to begin the hard tasks that will await us. The train rumbles southwards through the sleeping countryside. My fellow passengers are asleep. In other trains going to other corners of South India the other bishops are on their several ways. We have to turn our minds resolutely towards the task of making union a reality locally, meeting with patience and love the many forces that are for ever trying to divide men from each other, creating the necessary diocesan organization, knitting together the many different strands of separate life and labour, and above all keeping before every Christian mind the purpose of our union—'that the world may believe.' A huge task, but to-night everything seems possible. God grant us to be faithful in the days when nothing seems possible!

## THREE

THE first thing is to get into personal touch with the congregations. There are roughly five hundred and fifty of them, so one must begin with the main centres. But the union will mean nothing unless there can be personal contact. Plans for the next three months must include plenty of touring. It must be clear from the outset that a bishop is primarily a pastor, not a bureaucrat.

The second thing is to get a diocesan constitution hammered out. That will need long hours of committee work with plenty of time for drafting between. How far shall we be able to get agreement? The Diocesan Council must be constituted within three months to elect delegates to the Synod. All the same, visitation must come first.

# FOUR

THE country bus sways and jolts along the road, scattering the poultry, cattle and pedestrians in front and leaving a long cloud of white dust for a hundred yards behind. It is a ramshackle affair and there seems to be no reason why it should not fall to pieces at any moment. Inside it there is a close-packed cargo of men, women and children, baskets, sacks, boxes and babies. Those that don't get a seat squat comfortably on the floor. There is a continuous high-pitched crackle of conversation, easily heard above the roar of the engine. We do not talk about the weather or anything so trivial. Money, marriages, village gossip, religion, politics—these all have their share of attention. The stranger is thoroughly catechized. Occupation, native place, monthly income, father's name and income, destination, object of journey—these questions have to be answered by way of introduction. The last question leads out into theological territory where everyone can join in. Even the V.I.P.s in the front seat beside the driver turn round to cock an ear at the conversation. There is every variety of response from the open-eyed wonder of the villager who has never heard of the Gospel, to the blasé scepticism of the college graduate who has seen through it all. A prosperous-looking Brahmin begins a mocking imitation of a missionary preaching in Tamil: 'Ah, rascals, dolts, tramps and vagabonds, come to us and we will take you in.' Tamil has no words which really mean to 'save sinners.' Apart from Christ, how could it? The words in the Tamil Bible could equally be translated 'to provide free board and lodging for rascals.' That is one of the inescapable problems of evangelism. The Brahmin has made a good hit and gets a good laugh for it. I am wondering how to reply when an unexpected ally turns up. A young farmer, sitting on the bench behind, leans forward and tackles the Brahmin. 'I know all your nonsense. "All religions the same," you say. "All roads lead to God." It is not true. If you want to go somewhere you have to get into the right bus. If you get into the wrong bus you get to the wrong place. If you want salvation you have got to have the religion that gets you there. That's Christianity.' The Brahmin was not expecting this and is silenced. It is quite good fun teasing a missionary, but decidedly less edifying to argue about religion with an obvious outcaste. The farmer tells me his story, how he became a Christian, how he learned to be a good farmer, how he has developed fruit farming. Here is his place now. There are his fruit trees over there. He shouts to the driver to stop and gets down, shoulders his bundle, and tramps off through the fields to his house. The Brahmin is a little sorry for his attack and we have a good talk.

The bus is slowing up again at the signal of a group standing by the roadside. This is where I have to get down. The pastor, the village teacher, and some of the elders are waiting to greet me. The village deacon comes forward with one of the exquisitely beautiful garlands with which the Tamil expresses his greetings.

We walk together to the village. The path takes us over a low ridge and for a moment the view is limited to a steep slope of rough stones and pebbles fearsomely guarded by cactus and thorns of every description. Suddenly we are at the top of the steep path and look down at a scene of startling loveliness. A great sea of emerald green paddy fields stretches away from the foot of the hill. Dotted about it there are islands of trees, within each of which glimpses can be seen of houses and village streets, with here and there the graceful tower of a small village temple. In the group of trees nearest to us gleams the spotless white of a church tower, its top rising clear of the tree-tops and making a centre to which the eye again and again returns. In the middle distance the plain is broken by little rocky hills similar to the one we are standing on, and away to the west stands the great rampart of the Palni Hills rising to 8,000 feet and dwarfing into insignificance the hills in front of it. As we stand on the top of the hill the song of the men drawing water for the fields floats across to us for a moment, a slow, rhythmic sing-song keeping tune with the see-saw movement of the water-lift.

Then another sound sweeps up from the foot of the hill, the sound of instruments being tuned. Under the shade of a great tamarind tree the congregation is waiting for us, and they have spied us as we cross the hill. The drums are being heated over a hastily kindled fire of straw to tune them to the proper pitch, and the trumpeters are fitting the reeds into their long trumpets. The children are being hastily marshalled, their scores of little flags and banners fluttering in the breeze. As we approach, the band strikes up—a tremendous rattle of drums and a shrill wild melody on the pipes over a long sustained drone in the bass. As we approach and another garland is given the sound rises to a shattering climax. The drummers work up to a frenzy of furious beating, the sweat pouring down their bodies and their hair falling over their faces with the vigour of the dance. The cheeks of the trumpeters look as though they would burst at any moment. Two or three rockets are sent up just to add to the noise, the men and children clap their hands and the women give their greetings with a long high-pitched warbling cry which can be heard high above all the tremendous din.

Greetings over, we turn and walk in procession to the village, along the path between the paddy fields. The children sing a Christian lyric, not worrying apparently whether the sound is drowned by the band or not. With fluttering flags and pipe and drum we enter the narrow village streets. The rough sun-baked mud walls of the houses are only ten or twelve feet apart, and through the narrow gorge the human stream must somehow flow. The surging flood develops eddies. Small children nearly trip over the buffaloes sleeping peacefully outside their owners' front doors. Interested villagers join in, and increase the congestion. As we push and jostle along the sun beats down pitilessly from a cloudless sky, and the dust stirred up by hundreds of feet begins to choke the throat. Every doorway is crammed with spectators, men in their white loin-cloths, women in their brilliant sarees, their ears and noses heavy with massive gold rings, children, naked but for a string of beads, torn between fascination and terror, and clutching their mothers' sarees while they peep out from between their legs. We are all singing now, the 150th Psalm to a tune that makes one want to dance, and the procession swings along at a lively speed.

A burst of fireworks greets us as we come out into the open space in front of the church, and the bell peals out its contribution to the general din. A *pandal* of bamboo and leaves has been erected, and there is a banner which makes a fairly good attempt at spelling the name of the bishop. In a few minutes the whole village is crowding into the open space. With many shouts and slaps the children are being made to sit down and be quiet. The women stand in a big group at one side. The men are on the other, some sitting on the ground and some standing. There is an expectant hush.

The pastor opens with prayer. Some of the young men sing a lyric which they have composed for the occasion. A space is cleared in the centre and the small children give a beautiful display of *kummi* folk-dancing. Then with much impressive clearing of the throat one of the elders rises, unrolls a large scroll of paper, and proceeds to read. It expresses, with vast grandiloquence, the welcome of the congregation to its first bishop. Sonorous honorifics roll forth in a noble stream. The history of the congregation is recalled, its first founders and converts gratefully remembered, its present position described. Then, with a rather alarming change from allargando to staccato, there is a catalogue of current requirements to which the beneficent bishop will undoubtedly give his immediate attention: the well requires deepening, the school should be raised to the Higher Elementary Grade, the crack in the church tower should at once be repaired, failing which the tower will certainly fall down, and scholarships at one of the high schools should be provided for several children of the congregation. Finally, with many assurances of fervent devotion and prayer, the congregation members remain his Lordship's loving and obedient children. At this point there is a flourish of trumpets and a large tray of fruits, coconut, betel and sugar is ceremoniously presented along with yet another garland. The children relieve their pent-up feelings with a burst of loud applause. Another little procession comes in from the side with another tray of fruits and flowers; Hindus of the village also wish to present their greetings. This provides another opportunity for everyone to make a loud noise. Then there is a great silence again. The programme says 'Chairman's concluding remarks.' Now is the moment to preach Christ. God! let me know nothing among them save Christ and Him crucified! Let me placard the Cross here in the midst of this great and expectant crowd—not a crowd but a village, one living community—so that all of them, Hindus and Christians equally, may understand and believe! There is a wonderful starting point. I tell them about the union, how Christ died to draw all the children of God into one, how Satan entered in and divided the Church, how these divisions have remained unhealed for centuries, and how God has so wonderfully healed them here. I tell them how God has placed a special responsibility on us, how the Churches in the West are still hanging back, how we have been privileged to be allowed to go forward. I remind them of the things in our Church that make us unfit for this calling. And that brings us straight to penitence, to the atoning death for sinners, and to the challenge to repent and believe. Holy Spirit! take these words and make them living and powerful to the creating of faith!

The children are getting restless. I have been preaching for half an hour. The women are wanting to get back to their cooking. With prayer and a blessing the gathering is dismissed and the Christians are asked to be ready for service in an hour's time. My throat is dry and I am suddenly tired, but with the deep content that always follows the preaching of God's Word. The members come one by one to give their personal greetings, some to ask for special prayer for themselves and their children. The pastor and I promise to visit the sick and those in special need after church. The teacher and his wife are calling us to come to their house for tea and we thankfully go with them.

The hospitality of a Christian home in the midst of an Indian village is something wonderfully precious. The teacher's house, of course, is only an affair of mud and thatch with a doorway so low that one has to bend right down to enter. Apart from cooking vessels, mats and books there is hardly any furniture. His total income is less than £1 per week. Yet his house is the real centre of a manifold ministry to the whole village. How he does it is a mystery to me. Now he has prepared a meal for us of the tasty South India cakes, and a welcome cup of hot tea. We sit cross-legged on the floor and eat off plantain leaves while the teacher guards the door against interruptions and his good wife hovers around trying all the time to press us to take more.

As soon as tea is over the teacher does some whispering with the pastor. The latter comes over to say that two couples have come with babies whom they want the bishop to baptize. Why will people not give notice properly beforehand? They are invited in and we sit down on the floor to talk. Do they understand the meaning of what they are asking? Are they prepared to carry out the promises they must make? Have they any older children, and if so how have the baptismal promises been carried out in respect of them? The teacher reports that the elder children are regularly coming to the church and Sunday School, and that the families are good Christian families. I agree to baptize and go briefly through the service with the parents and we have prayer together.

By now the first bell has rung and the people are gathering in the church. It is a good solid piece of New England church architecture and its square, white tower easily dominates the village. Inside it is quite bare, with no seats and very little other furniture. The woodwork badly needs painting, but the whitewash is fresh and gleaming, and the whole building is gaily decorated with leaves. The people sit cross-legged on the floor—men on one side and women on the other, and children all together in front where the teacher can keep an eye on them. The group of young men who sang at the earlier meeting form a little choir at one side, and with violin, harmonium and small cymbals they are leading the congregation in praise while they wait for the second bell to ring. An oil lamp is brought in and hung from the roof, for it will be dark before we finish.

As we wait outside the teacher's house the bright evening sun is touching the water in the paddy fields to gold and everything is bathed in golden light. The small boys who tend the cattle are driving them slowly back from the fields through the narrow streets. The slow, lazy beasts amble down the streets, filling it with the many-toned tinkle of their bells, while the little boys urge them along with shouts and blows of their sticks. As each animal comes to its owner's house, it turns in at the door or waits patiently beside it, and soon the noise and the dust have settled. The sun's rim is touching the mountain rampart to the west, and the strange breathless hush of the moment of sunset descends upon the village. The bell peals out again and the sound of singing from the church ceases. For a moment the pastor and I stand together in the porch of the church while a few idle bystanders watch. 'Lord grant unto us Thy people to worship Thee in spirit and in truth and being nourished by Thy Word to be strengthened for Thy service, through Jesus Christ our Lord.' Then we go in.

The service is a very corporate affair. Most of the members have in their hands the little book which includes the prayers and lyrics in general use. Almost all except the very aged join heartily in prayer and praise.

How good it is to be able to use both 'fixed' and 'free' forms of prayer! The former provide the solid framework of the service and make it easy for everyone—however illiterate—to join in. The latter speak quickly to the heart and lift all together into the heavenlies. At the offertory we have what in Scotland would be 'the long prayer,' but Scotland would not produce that fervent 'Amen' from the whole congregation together. This sermon gives a chance to get close to the people and to test their grip on the Faith. The interplay of question and answer sustains the sense of a common act which has pervaded the whole service, and it is a delight to see some of the younger and better educated members with their Bibles in their laps, eager to be the first to find and read out the texts which are referred to. Alas—there are all too few who have Bibles. The Bible-famine of the war years is showing its results now, and those who are just leaving school have grown through those decisive years without Bibles in their hands. I must make it one of the first concerns to get into circulation as many thousands of Bibles as the Bible Society can spare. The service ends with a brief act of preparation for the service of Holy Communion to-morrow morning.

It is quite dark as we come out of the church. Everyone wants to have a word of greeting before leaving. A few hang about and appear to be unwilling to go. The teacher briefly explains that there are some difficulties to be thrashed out, so we agree to have a *panchayat* and try to settle them after paying the sick visits which had been promised.

The teacher leads the way with a little hurricane lamp, and a small group follows as we pick our way through the narrow passages between the mud huts. Above, the sky is a strip of deepest black spangled with brilliant stars and framed by the straw-roofs of two houses. Below, one has to pick one's way past sleeping cattle and over cobbles and filth. Through doorways as we pass we see the women blowing up the fires under the rice pots. The first call is to a Hindu named Mathu who cut open his foot with a digging mattock a few weeks ago. With proper treatment it would have been healed in a few days. Now he is lying on his bed in terrible pain, the foot a mass of stinking pus adorned with the dressing of the village 'doctor.' Why did he not go to the Mission Hospital? It is too far. We don't know anyone there. There is no one to recommend us. If it is God's will he will get better, so why go so far? But he has faith that if we pray to Jesus, He will cure him. His wife falls down and clutches our feet, beseeching us to pray for her husband. There is a long pleading and explaining, and at last they consent to let the teacher take him by bus to-morrow, and I write out a note of introduction to the doctor. Then we all kneel round the rough string cot and pray.

The next call is for Mariammal, a girl of seventeen troubled by a devil. When it seizes her she is like someone stupefied. Everyone knows that Jesus is able to cast out devils. When her sister was troubled the same way, young Jesudoss drove the devil away for ever in the name of Jesus. He was just a lad back from the Army then. Now he is completing his course in the

Training School. Mariammal is quite well at present, but her family want us to pray specially for her. Mariammal has real faith and listens eagerly as we read to her from the Gospel, and then kneels as I lay hands on her and we all pray for her.

The last call is to Abraham. He is an incurable case of tuberculosis. I gather he was a wild youth with a very bad reputation. Then he got T.B. and was sent to the Union Mission Tuberculosis Sanatorium. Later he was discharged as incurable. Now he is back in his village waiting to meet his Lord. The foreglow of the resurrection is already in his face. It is the kind of pastoral visit from which the pastor receives infinitely more than he gives. The light of the lamp is barely enough to lighten the little mud hut, and in the shadows one fancies that all the company of heaven are gathering. We pray not so much for Abraham as for the whole state of Christ's Church militant here in earth.

We now get back to the teacher's house. There is already quite a crowd gathered. It is going to be a long business. Two or three elders come with us into the church, and we all sit in a circle. The pastor leads in prayer. A rough, rebellious-looking man of about thirty-five stands on one side, and a little group with a woman in the midst on the other. Things begin very slowly. No one wants to speak. Nobody expects that anything significant will be said in the first half-hour. Slowly the pattern of the story becomes clear—a broken marriage, secret adultery, and now an open breach. Swamidoss has abandoned his wife and taken the other girl. Voices rise in accusation and counter-accusation, and rash speakers have to be sternly reminded that they are speaking in the presence of God. What is to be done? Before Christianity came it would be quite simple. Probably he would be fined forty rupees and the fine would be spent on providing toddy for the elders. One of the elders still can't think of anything different and suggests a fine. The others realize that that will not do, and that the Gospel makes a difference, but they are inarticulate about it. The pastor and I try to make Swamidoss understand both the evil of his ways and the possibility of pardon and restitution. For an hour we all plead, but it is like talking to a post. It seems as if the Cross means nothing to him. His wife weeps bitterly and her parents rail at the impotence of the Church to solve their problems. We have to confess absolute defeat. For the moment there is only one thing to do—to cast out the wicked member. With grief and bitterness of heart I tell Swamidoss that he is suspended from Holy Communion till the Pastorate Committee deals with the case, and that he must expect excommunication. He is dismissed and we try to comfort the forsaken wife. Together we pray for the unrepentant man, for his wife, and for the Church.

It is past ten o'clock, but we are not finished. There is trouble about the path that leads to the well. The Christians here are from the *Paraiyar* community and are not allowed to use the big well, but they have a small well built for them by the Government. The path to it leads past the *Pallar* quarter. The *Pallars* are fouling the path and obstructing its use. Three petitions have been sent to the Government without avail.

When the Revenue Inspector was camping in the next village they went on a deputation to him and he promised to look into it, but nothing was done. Yesterday one of the Christian women was threatened with assault when using the path. Will the bishop please speak to the Collector about it?

There is another matter. The Boys' High School at ——is in a very bad state and a positive hindrance to the Church. The bishop should look into it at once. A few minutes' probing and sifting brings us to the actual facts, which are that the eldest son of the village deacon who was studying in Form V last year has not been promoted to Form VI. The only possible explanation is that the Headmaster has a rooted prejudice against the Christians of this village and is determined to obstruct their advancement. For ten minutes I try, without much success, to explain that promotions really are based on examination results and not on personal favour, and that it will not be in the best interests of the Church to have it otherwise. Such objectivity is hard to achieve. The deacon is finally mollified by my invitation to his son to come and see me and talk about his future, and all is peace again. Everyone suddenly develops a tender solicitude regarding the bishop's hunger, and further problems are firmly refused a hearing. We kneel for a final prayer and blessing, and then the pastor and I thankfully go back to the teacher's house for food. It is midnight when I am finally stretched out in bed under the open sky. The sound of voices can still be heard from the church, and every now and then there is a furious outburst of barking as the village dogs fight over some scrap of refuse.

The next sound of which I am conscious is the bell at five o'clock. It is still quite dark. The teacher brings a bucket of water from the well, and I try to find a place where I can have a quick wash before the inevitable crowd of spectators gathers. Then into the church for the one period of the day when one is safe from interruption. By the time the second bell rings at six o'clock it is light enough to read, and the communicants are ready in church. They are a smaller group than last night. Some of them are on their knees at their private devotions. The pastor and I face the people from behind the Table, and the people come up to receive, except for the very aged and infirm who receive in their places. We close with the 23rd Psalm said all together before the final blessing, and then all go out to the day's work in field and house.

After breakfast the teacher has some matters he wants to talk about. There are two or three families who are completely indifferent about worship. They have been repeatedly warned, but take no notice. What can we do about them? There is a young man—a former pupil of the School—who wants baptism. He seems to be perfectly sincere. Will the bishop have a talk with him and encourage him? There is a man who ran away with a Hindu girl three years ago and has been living with her ever since. He was excommunicated at that time. Now he is sorry and wants to be restored. He is willing to confess his sins before the congregation publicly and ask for their pardon. Can he be restored? He is here and wants to speak. There is a woman whose husband went away three years ago to work in Singapore. At first he sent money regularly, but for eighteen months he has neither written nor sent money. There is a rumour that he has taken another girl. Will the bishop try to find out where he is and see that he comes back to his wife? Then the teacher is troubled about his son in the college. He has completed one year, but there is not enough money to finish the course. Is there any scholarship which he could get?

When these problems have been talked out it is time for school to begin. About eighty small boys and girls, mostly dirty and undernourished, are lined up round the mud-wall of the school building. They sing a Christian lyric and then the teacher leads them in prayer. The teacher and his wife preside at opposite ends of the little building, and manage to cope with five classes between them. I examine their Bible knowledge. It is shockingly bad. When pressed the teacher admits that he hasn't given any Scripture teaching since the last visit of the Government Inspector, who told him that he was not allowed to do it. This is something which will have to be tackled very firmly throughout the diocese.

The pastor reminds me that we have to catch a bus at ten-thirty for our next visit, and that the congregation will be expecting us. We say our good-byes and thanks to the teacher and his wife, and set off over the hill to the road. The village is very quiet compared to yesterday, for all but the very young and the very old are out in the fields. The sun is high in the sky, its hot glare destroying all the magic of the landscape and obliterating all its delicate contrasts. But it is cooler walking between the green paddy fields and watching the sparkle and splash of the water as it flows from the water-lift down the narrow channels hemmed with grass and delicate flowers. The men working the lift are some of the communicants of the morning, and greet us as we pass. They are stripped now, their clean white cloths tightly girt, and their dark bodies glistening with sweat. As we mount the bare hill, the hot glare of the sun is like the heat from an oven. Then as we cross the ridge the song of the water-lift dies away, and the strident noise of a motor horn greets us. We are late, and the driver is waiting for us. We hurry down to the road, thank the boy who has already put our luggage on the bus roof, and climb in.

## FIVE

FIVE hundred and fifty village congregations are going to take a lot of visiting. It is going to be important to keep the right balance between touring and the necessary work at home. It looks as if the best plan is to spend, roughly speaking, Friday to Monday in touring and Tuesday to Thursday at home. Four days of touring, including perhaps six or seven villages, is enough for one stretch. For one thing, one brings home from every tour problems which must be solved at home. For another, one cannot go on preaching five sermons for very long without a break.

Each village has its own very special character; yet they build up a sort of composite picture in the mind. Sitting on a string cot in a village street, watching a big crowd listening to the Gospel, I often find myself mentally trying to place this scene in a whole picture of the world. These South Indian villages have been a sort of vast human reservoir from which men have been recruited to do the hard and monotonous work of the world. On the tea and rubber plantations of Ceylon and Malaya, in the docks of Rangoon, Penang and Singapore, in South and East Africa, in the Andaman and Nicobar Islands, and even away in the Fiji Islands they are carrying on their strong shoulders the burdens of this complicated world. Yet here in these villages there is still a pattern of life not destroyed by the ferment of Western civilization. One can say that these villages belong to prehistory rather than to history. Or perhaps one should say that they are just emerging into history. It is true that they are touched at many points by the modern world-civilization. But their fundamental social pattern is still the ancient one, and even if Western civilization were to be blotted out by atomic warfare, I suppose that life here would not be profoundly changed.

The warp and the woof of the social fabric are the village and the caste. The village was, until not long ago, an almost self-contained economic unit which could function without the use of money. Each group within it had its place, and it was unthinkable that there should be any change. Each specialized worker received his remuneration not in money but in a share of land or its produce. Priest, carpenter, potter, washerman, barber, sweeper—each had his traditional perquisites and privileges, and the whole social structure was bound together by bonds of immemorial antiquity. Each group was a strictly separate endogamous group, yet each was bound socially and economically to the whole. Of course forces have been at work for many decades to disrupt this system. Products of modern industry have found their way into the village and stimulated new demands which could only be met with money. The thousands who have emigrated to towns and plantations have sent back a stream of money to their families at home. The postman with his sheaf of money orders is a significant figure for the social economy of the village. In recent years new factors have greatly accelerated the development of a money economy. The drastic fall in the value of money during the war years encouraged those who could do so to pay their dues in cash, and the appearance of ration shops in every village, with intensive efforts by the Government to bring all stocks of grain into the rationing system, makes it more and more necessary for the landless to have money in their hands. Yet, although the ancient bonds are so much loosened, the ancient pattern is not destroyed. The village is still an immensely strong and distinct social unit. The very appearance of the countryside proclaims that fact. Travelling through most of England one finds it hard to say where one town ends and another begins. Population is spread in a sort of uneven rash. There is nothing like that here. Each village stands by itself, surrounded by its fields, and in most cases the boundary that divides houses from fields has not changed for centuries. Each appears as distinct and as permanent as one of the islands in an archipelago.

The other strand in the social fabric is caste. Each village is a very distinct unit. But at the same time it is a composite structure, made up of distinct groups each living usually in a separate quarter of the village and each belonging to a larger community—the caste—where members are spread over thousands of similar villages. There are literally thousands of such castes, and each is an intensely cohesive community bound together by ties of blood, of a common occupation, and of innumerable common customs. Marriage outside the caste is normally unthinkable. The members of the caste feel themselves to belong to one another as brothers and sisters, and even though they may quarrel among themselves, they will display intense loyalty in standing by one another against the outside world. They share a host of common customs in dress, in idiom of speech, and in the ritual connected with birth, puberty, marriage and death, as well as a common occupation. Common ethical standards are maintained by the elders of the caste, and the ordinary man fears a *panchayat* of his own caste (which can finally out-caste him) more than a Government official who may merely send him to prison.

The ancient social fabric is thus one of great toughness and delicacy. Each man is set in two different relationships. He and his brothers and sisters form a unit in the village. That unit is related to the rest of the village by a complicated series of economic and social ties. At the same time it is related to hundreds of thousands of similar units in other villages, by blood and by an intense feeling of common kinship. The checks and balances which this dual relationship provides have kept Hindu society in a state of equilibrium for centuries.

Of course, like the village community, the caste system has been under heavy and damaging attack. Western progressive individualism has deeply undermined it. The rise of new occupations required by modern technical civilization has created larger and larger areas where caste is irrelevant. Nationalism has found in caste an enemy that must be attacked. And the Christian conviction about the worth of every man, operating in various degrees of dilution through thousands of village schools, has discredited the system in the minds of those to whom it gave the lowest places. The new constitution makes discrimination on grounds of caste illegal, and many honest efforts are made to remove the evils of the system.

Yet the ancient system is still enormously strong. It is true, for instance, that in a normal village a member of the untouchable groups can now walk through the streets of the higher castes without punishment; many of the most degrading features of untouchability are being removed. But when one touches matters concerning food, drink and marriage, one discovers how immensely strong the system still is. I am constantly asked to help untouchable groups to get permission for the use of wells. On one occasion I was so foolish as to approach the caste people on their behalf. With as much delicacy as possible I spoke of the terrible difficulties of the outcaste group who were compelled to collect their water in a muddy pool, into which filth from the refuse heaps was constantly draining, while there was a fine deep well close by which they were not allowed to use. The only result of the conversation was that, when I left, the caste people raided the outcaste quarters and beat up the people there. A social pattern which has determined the whole life for so many centuries cannot be suddenly abolished. It is bound to exercise a profound influence for many generations.

But we are still at the dawn of history here in these villages. A tremendous ferment is at work and it is impossible to predict the future. Surely it is of immense significance that the Church has become rooted here, right in the villages, and among the lowest strata of society. In the West the Church is largely middle-class: here it is chiefly rooted among the labourers. Communism is appearing in the villages, but it is the Gospel which has created the ferment and which still has the greater hold. Moreover the thousands of Christians who have gone as labourers to cities and plantations all over South-East Asia and beyond have taken their faith with them, and have in many places founded new Churches where they have settled. Something like a truly indigenous Christian culture is to be found here, though it is not what is often sought for by that name. The Gospel is here present and operative at what looks like a vital growing point in human history.

Inevitably the spread of the Gospel has been along the channels provided by social structure. Caste groups have moved together and have spread the good news to their brethren of the same caste in other villages. Because their position in the structure of the village is not changed by their becoming Christians, they are still apt to think of themselves as belonging to their caste, especially if a large number have become Christians together. If there are Christians of other castes in the same village, the character of the Church as a community transcending caste becomes clear and challenging, and there are immediate ethical problems to be faced and settled. If, as is unfortunately often the case, the congregation in one village is all from one caste, it is much more difficult to make the nature of the Church clear. There is nothing obvious to challenge the assumption that the old natural community remains. Yet eventually the Church, as a totally new kind of community, must challenge the older form of community, and a painful tension is set up. It is part of the mission of the Church to set up such a tension. It must not evade it either by seeking to deny and repudiate all the ties of kinship, or by capitulating to them and allowing them to have control. It must demonstrate its character as something of a wholly different order.

It is here that the issue of unity becomes so clear. In some parts of South India where two missions have competed for the allegiance of the same villages, there are now two churches in each village each consisting of converts from one caste. The old caste-division is now camouflaged by a fine display of conviction about theological principles. In such a situation the Church contradicts its own nature. On the other hand, where one church stands in the village, claiming the allegiance of all and binding all by common bonds to one Lord, the true character of the Church becomes clear. At the same time the Church becomes involved in tremendous tensions, and often, alas, in very bitter and un-Christian quarrels.

## SIX

BETWEEN tours, time has to be found both for correspondence and for the committee work required to get the diocesan organization functioning. We are making good progress. At the beginning a decision was made not to vote but to work for agreement. This creates the right atmosphere and prevents any feeling that the ex-Anglican minority might be out-voted by the large ex-Congregationalist majority. The best part of the work has been the small drafting committees where the different traditions are ably represented. It is extraordinarily interesting and rewarding, this process of coming to grips with traditions quite different from one's own, and seeking to test everything by fundamental Scriptural principles. Of course the general outline is laid down by the Scheme of Union, but there is a vast amount of detail to be filled in, and it is in regard to these details that people's ordinary concerns and interests are involved. Who is to have a voice in the location of presbyters? What power is the congregation to have in the matter? Who is to have a right to vote in church elections, and to sit on Pastorate Committees? How are the principals of schools and colleges, heads of hospitals, District Council Chairmen and the rest of them to be appointed or elected? How can we guard against intrigue and 'church politics' and yet retain a large element of democracy? How is the bishop's authority to be related to that of various councils and committees? How is the discipline of ordinary church members to be administered? What is to be the position of the Church *vis-à-vis* the foreign missionary societies in regard to control of work, appointment and posting of missionaries and use of grants? These and dozens of similar questions have to be faced and some kind of answer given in the first three months of our existence as a diocese.

It is interesting to notice the way different traditions reveal themselves in the course of argument and counter-argument. The ex-Anglican members have a strong sense of the authority of the Church in spiritual matters, and of course of the dignity of the bishop's office. Along with it they are very keen on a large lay-participation in the management of the financial and administrative affairs of the Church—often seeming to suggest that these can be entirely divorced from the 'spiritual.' 'We manage the financial affairs: we leave spiritual matters entirely to the bishop and clergy,' is a remark often heard, and it takes time to explain why this absolute separation is wrong. The ex-Congregationalists, on the other hand, have a strong sense that the whole life of the Church is the concern of its whole membership, but a weak sense of the authority of the Church. Some speak as though a church constitution was something one could make *de novo.* At the last meeting I put a large Bible on the table and pointed out that our constitution was already there, and we were only making local rules. I intend to have it there at every meeting as a reminder. Having accepted episcopacy some are ready to tumble over themselves in putting everything into the hands of the bishop, and it is frequently necessary to insist on the equal importance of the other elements in the whole life of the Church. Oddly enough it was necessary to insist—against congregationalist opposition—that the holding of at least one congregational meeting per year should be obligatory.

Then there are those for whom independence has made all things new, so that all suggestion of personal authority is met with the statement, 'In free India we cannot allow anything that is not completely democratic.' Immediately the experience of some school principal, whose work has been made intolerable by intrigue and place-hunting, is thrown back as a counter-argument, and then we slowly work back and forth through concrete examples down to the basic biblical principles. How far is the idea of democracy applicable to the Church and how far is it not? How is the final authority of Christ Himself mediated through the daily life of the Church? Always in the background there are strong personal feelings, or the memories of such feelings. There is no escaping from the problem of power. The modern District Council Chairman fills the position of the old District Missionary, and he inherits much of his power. But whereas in the old days the missionary was hardly conscious that he was wielding autocratic power over the lives of hundreds of people—to-day everyone is very conscious indeed of the power which his successor wields. The principal of a school or college, again, wields power over the future of the children of most of the members who are sitting on this committee. In a situation where many educated Christians look naturally for employment in the large Christian institutions, the question who is to be the person who controls these institutions is one that touches everyone's immediate interests very closely. So we are not discussing abstract questions. We are trying to bring true theology to bear upon very concrete personal interests.

The Church inherits from the missionary societies which began it an immense programme of educational and medical work. In relation to the resources of the Western Churches this programme is perhaps not large, but in relation to the resources of the Indian Church it is immense. Consequently the primary work of the Church—the ministry of the Word and Sacraments—tends to be overshadowed by the business of managing this great volume of work. Ministration is swallowed up in administration. Yet the problem cannot be evaded by cutting the educational and medical work loose and letting it steer its own course. Whatever may be true in a country of preponderantly Christian traditions, in a non-Christian country that is simply to invite destruction by absorption. The younger Church has to take the responsibility given to it by the older. The alternative of leaving the Western Churches the responsibility for control is no longer possible or desirable. Yet there is a terrible danger that the Church should become a large social service organization with its centre in a modern streamlined office rather than God's family with its centre in 'the apostles' teaching and fellowship, the breaking of bread and the prayers.' The problem comes to a head in the question of the place and work of the bishop. Just because there is so much to do in the realm of organization, the temptation will be to accept the place into which the whole of modern culture seems to conspire to push one—the office chair. This is a really vital point. A right stand here at the very start will help to reverse that trend which already makes most pastors love honour and desire a drawerful of files far above a shelfful of books.

## SEVEN

COMING back from evening service at the church last night I passed two processions. One was the familiar kind—an idol on a great throne carried on the shoulders of a couple of score of men, sweating and struggling and shouting under the terrific weight, glaring power lights and guttering torches, Brahmins chanting slogans from the Vedas, the clatter and shriek of drum and pipes and a motley, shapeless crowd following. The other one was the kind that is becoming more and more familiar—a Communist demonstration. A rigidly disciplined crowd of several hundred marched four abreast along the street. There was no music, only the terrific unison roar of the slogans directed by the leaders. They had been worked up into a sort of frenzy, and the roar was more like that of beasts than any human sound. This morning there are notices chalked up on all the walls, calling for a strike of the mill workers. The Communists have got control of the mill-workers' union.

The Utopia that was to come with freedom has not appeared. Thousands of people, for instance, thought that Free India would not expect poor people to pay for their railway journeys, and the railway police are being kept busy. Six million people were detected travelling without tickets on the railways in the first year of independence. The great achievements of Government in dealing with the appalling aftermath of partition, in tackling the problems of the great *zemindari* estates, and in introducing and enforcing prohibition, and their efforts to tackle other abuses, are easily forgotten by the politically uneducated. The world has not changed overnight as they expected it to do. The Communists are making very successful use of this. It is easy for cynics to point to the moral deterioration which Congress has suffered since it could offer jobs to its loyal members instead of jail. Corruption is everywhere. All this provides excellent opportunities for the Communists, who are hard-working, disciplined and well-organized. They are capturing both students and workers at a rapid rate. Moreover while their methods are quite unscrupulous, many of their activities can only be praised. They are waging a thoroughly justifiable campaign to force the landlords to give a larger share of the rice crop to the cultivators. At present the cultivator provides labour, bulls and ploughs, seed, manure and everything else, and gets one-third of the crop. The landlord, who may never even see his land, gets two-thirds. The Communist demand is that the cultivator should receive one-half. I don't think a Christian can do other than heartily approve of this demand. A wealthy landlord was very angry with me for saying so in the train the other night.

Unfortunately a good many Christians – both students and workers–are falling for the Communist propaganda. A leading member of the S.C.M. has become a Trotskyist. Many of the Christian mill workers have joined the Communist-sponsored union, a few from conviction, some because of personal differences with the leader of the other union, some simply because it is apparently the winning side. My efforts to tackle this issue with some of the Christians among the mill workers have so far failed. We don't have–so far as I know–a single page of Christian literature in Tamil dealing with the issue.

It is a tragedy that at this moment we should have the worst famine for many years. Whole areas are being almost depopulated as the people go elsewhere in the hope of food and work. It is pathetic to see them on the move, with children and a few cooking vessels, trudging along the roads, or crowding the station platforms. With so many million people living permanently on the edge of starvation, a single failure of the rains can push them over the edge. The organization of relief supplies, sent by the American Churches, is rapidly becoming one of the main jobs. It is a wonderful way of showing people what the Holy Catholic Church means.

## ✣ EIGHT ✣

I SPENT this morning at M. High School, seeing round the classes and talking things over with the principal. The immediate occasion was a new Government order about religious education in schools. It looks as if the Christian Education Council would have to take it up with Government on behalf of all the Christian schools. This vast educational programme of ours needs constant vigilance if it is to serve its real purpose. We have two colleges, six high schools, three training schools, two industrial schools and about one hundred and sixty ordinary elementary schools. Other dioceses have many more. The schools conducted by the Church of South India alone must run well into four figures. It is no use denying that they are an area of tension between Church and Government. It cannot be otherwise. It is important that this tension should not break out in unnecessary conflict. Government pays us big grants, and naturally exercises more and more control.

The control is sometimes wooden and unimaginative. We too easily become part of a system in which any real development of intelligence and judgment is crushed out. We intended to give an education centred in the Christian revelation. In fact we have more and more tended simply to teach a Government-imposed syllabus, with Bible added. Our schools have been evangelizing agencies, but their witness has certainly not been as clear as it should be. Now Government is severely restricting our right to teach the Bible. We must accept and welcome the principle that religious instruction is not to be given to a child without the consent of the parent. But we must constantly resist and expose the fallacy that 'education' is neutral and 'religion' an optional extra. That is where our real danger lies. It is an enormous advantage that this educational work is directly under the Church, so that its value is constantly being assessed from the point of view of the Church's central task. But there is need of much support for and fellowship with the teachers who are actually working day by day on this vital frontier of the Church.

One must sympathize with the difficulties of Government. In a country where conflict between religions has wrought such evil, the policy of religious neutrality is plainly the only right one. But two factors combine to give to that policy a definite twist against Christian evangelism. One is the immense and all-pervasive influence of the Vedanta philosophy, an influence which colours all thinking in this country. The absolute monism of the Vedanta destroys in advance all claims on behalf of any religion for the allegiance of all men. To those who are under the influence of the Vedanta, Christian evangelism is an intolerable assertion of ultimate truth on behalf of one among the many forms of illusion. Activities aimed at conversion from one religion to another are both an offense against the ultimate truth of man's existence, and also destructive of the ordered harmony of social life based upon the proper performance by every man of the duties of his station. For the vast majority of our well-educated contemporaries the attempt to persuade a man to change his faith is something that arouses the deepest hostility and disgust. The second factor is the spread of secularism which, equally with the Vedanta, treats religious claims as irrelevant to the salvation of mankind.

These two factors powerfully reinforce one another. Their effect is that 'religious neutrality' becomes a determination to push religion to a harmless place at the periphery of life, in which syncretism appears as much a necessity of state as it did to the Roman Empire. Significantly these developments are accompanied by an unprecedented spate of official moral uplift. Almost every Governmental utterance is a sermon exhorting the people to put the development of moral character in the first place in all their efforts. Against this background it is galling to have to submit, for instance, to a Government officer demanding a search in a high school hostel to see if Hindu or Muslim boys are secreting Bibles and prayer-books. In this situation it may be the function of Marxism to force the issue of religious truth into the open.

# ✤ NINE ✤

Now that I have a car I am getting round the diocese more rapidly. That means, among other things, that I can take far more confirmations, a privilege for which I am very thankful. I am more and more impressed with the necessity of pushing up the general conception of what church membership involves. In some places it has fallen very low. How can one meet the disciplined ranks of the Communists with an undisciplined rabble not seriously committed to anything? This is a place where a bishop can really exert a steady pressure towards raising the standards. It is a joy to be able to forget the office for five days and concentrate on a purely pastoral job.

I have to leave the car at B. in the spacious yard of a wealthy Muslim gentleman's house. A year or two ago he built and equipped a whole village and settled twenty Christian families in it to work on his land. He provided them with a small church and insists that they attend worship regularly. He is himself a student of the Bible, though in my talk with him to-day I am not really able to get to grips with him in the realm of personal faith. He kindly supplies a bullock cart for the rest of the journey drawn by a very fine pair of bulls, and in a few minutes we are covering the rough country track at a good five miles per hour.

After about an hour we reach P., where a big crowd is waiting—the congregation of five nearby villages.

There is the usual reception, and then we go in procession with pipe and drum, this time preceded by two young men doing the local form of fencing. It is a sort of formalized fighting done with staves six feet long and must require very good training. To-day's display is really thrilling to watch, and I wish I could get a film taken of it.

The church is too small for the congregation, and as the afternoon sun is too hot for sitting in the open, we meet under an enormous pipal tree. Drinks are provided of the delicious cool water of the green tender coconut, and then we have a reception and address to the whole congregation along with Hindus from the village. Then the confirmation candidates go with me across the fields to the little church for an hour together. These hours with the young people just before their confirmation are extraordinarily precious. It is not primarily that they give an opportunity for testing their preparedness, though that is important. The main thing is that one can get into really vital contact with a group of young people at a decisive moment in their lives. To-day's group comes from several villages and is of varying degrees of preparedness. There are ten young men from T. prepared by a volunteer—a Government school teacher. They have a real understanding of what they are doing and there is a light in their eyes which leaves one in no doubt about their preparedness. The girls have been prepared by the Bible-women, and there is no doubt about them. There are a few who are not really ready. The teacher at M. has not been doing his job, and his lads will have to be told to wait.

Under the pipal tree the congregation soon assembles again. There is an intense hush which extends even to the casual bystanders on the edge of the crowd. This is the first episcopal confirmation in the neighbourhood. It must be confessed that admission to communicant membership has been in recent years a much less serious affair than it ought to have been, and this solemn service clearly goes home to the hearts of the people. After the questions and addresses we all kneel and sing a lovely Tamil lyric invoking the transforming power of the Holy Spirit. Everyone knows it, for it was composed by a well-loved pastor in these parts not many years ago, and all join quietly in the singing. Then there is a deep silence throughout the congregation as hands are laid with prayer on the head of each, while they kneel in their places. Prayer and praise conclude the service, and at the end it is almost dark. The congregation is dismissed with a blessing, and I invite the communicants only to follow me across the fields again to the little church. A small hurricane lamp guides us, and we sing as we go. Inside the church there is just room for all the communicants kneeling together on the earthen floor. It is a very crude building, and the thatch roof badly needs repair. Inside, the light of the small lamp is barely sufficient for reading. But one could not ask for a more fitting setting for the Lord's Supper. With deep joy and peace we receive this group of young people to be very members incorporate with us in the mystical Body of Christ.

Late at night there is a fine display of dancing and singing with the new book of Christian *Kummies*.

These attractive folk-dance tunes are so easily learned and remembered that they are an obvious vehicle for teaching, and we have now got a book of about forty songs set to them. They include Old and New Testament stories, the lives of our Lord, St. Paul and St. Peter (this being set to a popular fisherman's shanty), the story of creation, the Ten Commandments and many others. Even the dullest villagers pick them up quickly, and many of the congregations have learned to sing and dance them beautifully. Some of the words are, of course, not suitable for dancing at all, and sometimes there are errors of taste in this matter. But it is worth having a few occasional crudities for the sake of printing the Gospel story indelibly on the minds of people who will never learn in any other way.

There are a lot of village problems to be talked out before bedtime—mostly concerned with the ravages of some of the criminal tribes in the neighbourhood. Famine is making them bolder in their robberies.

Confirmations have been arranged at four centres, but even so there will be a great many left out. The figures show that out of about 1,200 adult Christians in the pastorate, 280 are still unconfirmed. On this tour only 100 at the outside will be confirmed. It is not likely that I can come back within a year. That seems a solid reason for encouraging continuance of confirmation by presbyters also. Comparison between the ex-Anglican and ex-Congregationalist pasorates shows that in the former the proportion of confirmed persons is considerably lower than in the latter. But the standard of preparation for confirmation is certainly higher in the former. Many people in the ex-Congregationalist pastorates seem to have been admitted to communion with no real preparation at all. That is a strong argument for the sort of common standard which episcopal confirmation secures. But it is a very grave defect in the Church when one-third of its adult members are not communicants, as is the case in the ex-Anglican pastorates. The Congregational churches have been accustomed to admitting new members to full communicant status at the normal Sunday morning service. This has obvious pastorate advantages. But clearly the bishop cannot always be present on a Sunday. It seems to me certain that the practice of episcopal confirmation will become general, but it will obviously be harmful to try to force it. The immediate task is to apply steady unremitting pressure in the direction of much more thorough and serious preparation. And that means more and more consecrated workers for the village congregations.

## TEN

THE sun is already very hot at nine o'clock, and the black cotton soil country through which we are passing offers little beauty to relieve the harsh glare. Once we pass a small tank, with an ancient, half-ruined temple beside it, and have a glimpse of the vivid grace of lotus blossom rising from water that reflects the intense blue of the sky. Here and there the oleander is in flower beside the road. But for the most part the country looks like its name—the robber country—a bleak, bare place where if there be anything of value it has been well hidden away. It is true that things have changed since systematic efforts to reclaim these criminal tribes began. Most of them have—at least officially—given up their ancient occupation and begun to settle down as cultivators. But generations of hereditary skill are not easily put aside, and I am told that it is still true in many places that a man's chances of winning a bride depend upon the valour and daring of his robberies.

Until recently the reclamation work was in the hands of Christian missions, and though the schools are now directly under Government, a large proportion of the teachers are Christians. Very many have been trained at our training schools, and some of them can tell moving stories of Christian witness in this Robber Land.

We are turning off the main road now, and before long we reach a point where the car can go no further. A short walk brings us to K., and the little congregation gives us a great welcome. It is a day of pride and joy for David, the Government school teacher by whose witness this fine group was won for Christ. He began about three years ago, when he was working in this village, to gather the young men together each evening to study the Bible. For many months this daily study went on, and eventually David's prayers were answered and the young men gave themselves to Christ. But there were many difficulties to be faced. First was the absolute refusal of their wives to have anything to do with the new religion. To every entreaty they turned a deaf ear, and finally it became clear that the men would have to proceed to baptism without their womenfolk. Then there was the question of building a church. For weeks and weeks they tried to find a site, but every way seemed closed. One evening in a mood of desperation they met together and were praying most earnestly that God would show them His will in the matter, when a man came in and offered them a small plot, just big enough to build a small prayer house. With some help from a missionary, and with their own labour, they built the little church which we are now entering.

The day of their baptism brought a new trial. When they returned from the nearby town where the baptism had been held they found the doors of their houses barred against them. Their wives had met together in their absence and resolved upon a sort of boycott. They refused to cook their husbands' meals, to let them into the houses, or even to speak to them. For three days the newly baptized men fasted and waited and prayed. Their Hindu friends took pity on them and offered to feed them. They replied that if their wives would not feed them they would starve. After three days the women relented to the extent of agreeing to cook for them. But they refused to have any other dealings with their husbands, and waged a sort of cold war for many days. The men met this with patience and prayer. At last, after several months, their patience was rewarded. The women surrendered and confessed that they, too, needed the same Saviour. A period of preparation followed. Now the pastor has asked me to baptize them, and the service is fixed for to-morrow. At the same time the men are to be confirmed. To-day I am meeting with them to examine them and to have some personal talk with them before the service.

We squat cross-legged on the earth floor, the pastor beside me, and the women in a circle. They are a formidable looking group. They have the Amazonian build and fierce appearance of their tribe, and—as is customary—their ears are heavy with gold ornaments which draw down the lobes in a fantastic loop two inches below the natural limit. They do not take very kindly to my catechizing. They have had no Bible-woman to teach them, and some of them find it difficult to steer a straight course through the Lord's Prayer and the Ten Commandments. At one point the pastor loses patience with me and bursts out in English, 'Don't you understand that you are talking to a tamed tigress?' Looking at the lady opposite me I have to admit that it is a good description. Then one of the group of men who have been watching joins in. 'You can trust us,' he says. 'We shall see to it that they become good Christians.' I know that there is solid ground for that promise. The decisive thing has been done. They have turned from idols to serve the living God and to wait for His Son from heaven. I shall baptize them to-morrow.

# ✣ ELEVEN ✣

Holy Week begins round the annual performances of the Passion Play—*Love Divine*. As usual thousands of people have flocked in from town and village, and the great open-air theatre is packed and overflowing. I have come across many evidences of the evangelistic power of this dramatic presentation of the Gospel story, and I have been very eager to see it. The preparation and presentation of the play occupies a central part in the life of the community at P., and it is easy to sense the spirit of devotion and prayer which sustains the effort.

The vast audience is held in the grip of the story, and at the end the impression is overwhelming. It is surely impossible for anyone to see this without saying Amen in his heart to the witness of the Centurion—'Surely this Man was the Son of God.' Even though every detail of this story is so familiar, this fresh presentation of it through a new medium overwhelms all one's defences. Now that I have seen it, I understand some of the testimonies I have heard.

## TWELVE

This is one of the mornings when one longs for the bourgeois security of a front door and a bell. At home in Britain one seems to live most of life behind doors, and if people want to break in, they have to ring a bell and open a door. Here all doors have to be kept open, and there is no place where people cannot easily walk in. After five days on tour there is the usual huge pile of letters to be answered, but there seems to be little chance of even getting them read. Already at 7 a.m. there is a small queue. Daniel from M. comes with a letter from his pastor asking me to assist him in getting a job in the police. They are enlisting new men today, and if I put in a word for him he will have a good chance. A deputation from P. comes with the news that they have been ordered to remove the new prayer house within three days because it has been erected without getting the permission of one of the municipal departments which should have been consulted. An urgent letter is sent in by the pastor at N. to say that there has been an outbreak of rioting in one of the villages of his pastorate. Several Christian homes have been burned down. The help of the police is urgently required. Poor Mrs. B., whose husband was dismissed from employment because he was believed (probably rightly) to have Communist sympathies, is here again to plead with tears that I will somehow get him back his job. And there are two or three of the usual hard cases which seem, God help me, just completely insoluble.

By ten o'clock, and after a prolonged visit to the police headquarters, the queue has been somehow dealt with, and I start on the letters. There is the usual crop of petitions. Those in Tamil sometimes take a good deal of deciphering. The first paragraph can usually be omitted, for Tamil is a flowery language and the introductory address need not be taken seriously. But the main argument of the letter, often written by someone barely literate and under the stress of strong emotion, is apt to be extremely involved and tortuous. 'My father-in-law's great-uncle was the owner of three acres of wet land in Sivaganga Taluk. After the death of the first wife he married a second time and had five sons. By his first wife he had four sons and three daughters. In his will he divided the land as follows . . . It became necessary for my father-in-law's uncle to file a suit against——. Owing to our ill luck the suit was unsuccessful. . . . A further suit was filed by ——. I request you to settle the dispute between my wife and my brother-in-law to see that the land is restored to my wife. You are responsible for all Christians in this diocese, and it is clearly your duty to see that justice is done immediately.' 'With unutterable grief we beg to inform you about our Presbyter Rev. ——. Before he came here our church was peaceful, but now it is full of quarrels. He does not have the necessary tact to solve our quarrels. He has not given a proper account of the money subscribed at the last meeting of the Sisters Association. On Tuesday, 28th

March, he attended the cinema in ——. There are many of us who can prove it. He thus wastes his time in worldly pursuits and neglects the flock committed to him. Please arrange to transfer him to any other pastorate and send us a suitable pastor.'

Here is one impeccably typed in English with copies sent to most of the district officials. 'Notice given by —— most respectfully, sheweth: You better know about myself and my wife already before many years she is not in good terms with me. Many *panchayats* were held before the Rev. Father and I had her having sympathy for the girl. She never thought of it. On 30.10.47, without hearing any notice saying some bad temperful words she went away to her place. I wrote many times by post and send news through persons but received no reply. It is but nature that a man has to undergo meterimonial life for his full convenience but on my sake I lead a sagical life even though I was married. Afterall I have to say that my wife must return to me with all sorts of dowries including Rs. 100/- worth of jewells within the 20th January or with a statement before Rev. Father stating that she will be under my control. Failing which you must know certainly that this is the divorce notice without any kind of relationship to the wealth and lift among us. Your affectionately.' How much of this is the work of the typist and how much represents the poor man? I suppose it is a good thing to have one place where all the sorry wreckage of the Church's disorders can be washed up. God grant the power of healing and repair!

Fortunately there are plenty of other things in the

mail. There is routine correspondence of all kinds of constructive work, evangelistic, educational, medical and pastoral. The Council Chairman from A. writes that he took out a band of workers to the big Hindu festival in a nearby village, preached to hundreds of people and sold 850 Gospels and New Testaments. He wants a fresh supply, as he is sold out. A group of families in a village near M. has decided for Christ and asked for instruction and baptism. Can we send a good catechist? For the present a volunteer is working. Plans are being made for a retreat for factory workers in the area most heavily indoctrinated with Communism, and a strong group of young workers are supporting the plan enthusiastically. Old Appadurai, the ex-deacon of B. village, who had to be excommunicated last year and who seemed then to be as stubborn as a post, has at last repented. He has confessed his sin before the congregation and asked forgiveness, and the Pastorate Committee recommends him for restoration. Joy in heaven and on earth.

There are other—less happy—letters dealing with church discipline. Two Pastorate Committees send in formal reports on the trial of offenders and request orders of suspension from Communion in each case. The Pastorate Committee at B. has, on my formal instructions, investigated the charge that Mr. T.—a very influential member of the church—has arranged a bigamous marriage for his daughter. The committee finds the charge true, but confines itself to expressing its regret. Evidently the influence of Mr. T. weighed more with the Pastorate Committee than the fear of

God. They will have to be firmly told to meet and think again quickly or else that the case will be referred to the Court of the Diocese. The presbyter at M. reports that Mr. L., who was suspended from Holy Communion six months ago for using foully insulting language to a neighbour, is anxious to be restored. The pastor is not convinced of his repentance. The majority of the Pastorate Committee wants to impose a fine. One of the difficulties is that three of the Committee members are his close relatives. What advice is to be given?

The exercise of church discipline is one of the matters which union has effected on both sides of the diocese. It is one of the places where the mutual interdependence of the congregational, presbyteral and episcopal elements in the healthy ordering of the Church's life becomes extremely clear. In a certain sense we may say that the only place where truly Christian discipline can be exercised at all is in the congregation. The local congregation meeting regularly face to face, gathering round the same Table to break the same bread and drink the same cup, is the basic unit of the Church's life in a way nothing else can ever be. If love of the brethren does not exist here, it does not exist at all. Therefore it is here alone that Christian discipline can really be exercised. The exercise of it is in many ways the severest test of a church's Christianity. It is easy—fatally easy—for a congregation simply to shut its eyes to the sins of its members and to do nothing about them. It is also easy for it, under certain circumstances, to adopt a hard legalistic attitude which is without redemptive power. It is also very easy for a congregation to have so little spiritual unity that the exercise by it of disciplinary powers becomes hopelessly confused with the quarrels of individuals or groups and therefore fails to achieve its first end, which is the hallowing of God's Name. These failures have been constantly repeated in all churches. In the former Congregationalist part of this diocese the effect has been that in many places all serious and deliberate attempt to exercise church discipline was given up. On the other hand, it is not a solution to take the responsibility entirely off the shoulders of the congregation and place it upon those of a bishop. Action by a remote authority over the heads of the local congregation does not and cannot achieve the full ends of Christian discipline.

Union has meant at this point the re-uniting of things which ought never to have been separated. It is abundantly clear that St. Paul did not act over the head of the Corinthian church. He used his apostolic authority to make that church do the thing which only it could do. The whole authority of Christ in His Church was in the action of the apostle and the local congregation acting together ('ye being gathered together, and my spirit, with the power of our Lord Jesus'). To ex-Anglican congregations I find that I have again and again to write insisting that the local Pastorate Committee shall first take the responsibility and make its recommendation. To ex-Congregationalists I have to insist that fear of trouble must not prevent straight dealing with offenders, and to remind Pastorate Committees all the time that they are acting locally for the whole

Body of Christ and not as the officers of a local society. In every case where serious action is called for, the Pastorate Committee, the presbyter and the bishop all have a vital part to play. And the public act of excommunication is done *in* the congregation by reading the written proclamation of the bishop. Similarly, when restoration takes place—as, thank God, it often does—it is before the whole congregation that forgiveness has normally to be asked and given, and the whole congregation gathered for its public worship is party to the reception and restoration of the penitent. And where the local Pastorate Committee manifestly fails in its duty, appeal can at once be made the Court of the Diocese, where presbyters and lay members from other pastorates sitting under the chairmanship of the bishop can seek humbly to bring to bear upon a difficult local situation the mind of Christ.

While I am struggling to get essential letters ready for the post, another queue seems to have collected. It is 3 p.m. and the temperature is over a hundred degrees. A family from a village out on the dry eastern side of the diocese is waiting pathetically on the verandah. Father, mother, three children, all are terribly emaciated. The wells are dry, there is no work, no food and no hope. They have no special request, but simply want to be able to lay these unbearable burdens down. There are two others—village lads—searching for employment but with little hope. A wandering Christian preacher 'entirely independent of any Church' wants a license to preach throughout the diocese. He is one of a large and increasing class of men who live by wandering from church to church—some of them true servants of God, many of them the castaways of the Churches, some charlatans and imposters. It takes time and patience to learn which group each one belongs to. Another poor girl whose husband has deserted her is here with her parents demanding that I should solve the problem on the spot, and there is the usual series of requests for letters recommending sons and daughters for jobs or interviews. It is very, very hard to make people understand that one should speak the truth even in a letter of recommendation. After fifteen minutes' futile argument with a doting parent, I begin to think of the Bible Class this evening for which I have not yet prepared, and of the letters which positively must go by today's post at four o'clock. A hot wave of indignation and self-pity begins to mount in my brain and to spill out in my speech. Where have this morning's resolves about patience gone to? A vivid picture is flashed into my mind—a picture of the pastor's house at M. where I spent a day and a night recently. All day and practically all night his tiny little house of two rooms was surrounded by the people of the village, ceaselessly demanding, quarrelling, arguing, claiming as their right the Christian courtesy and patience that he was offering them as God's gracious gift. I remember thinking, after twenty-four hours, that a week of it would drive me mad. But he and his good wife never lost their patience for a moment. I look round at my large and airy bungalow. Truly I have a lot to learn from these whom I try to teach. The self-pity has ebbed as suddenly as it came, and I feel ashamed. I apologize and try to start again. But it is still hard to explain that one must speak the truth. And the post goes out at four o'clock.

## THIRTEEN

DURING the first few months I was trying to pay brief visits to as many centres as possible so as to establish a direct personal contact with the widely scattered congregations, especially with those which had not had a bishop before. Now there is time for more systematic visitation, pastorate by pastorate. This week-end I am in one of the ex-S.P.G. pastorates. They are small enough to make it possible to visit every village. When a pastorate has thirty to forty village congregations one abandons the attempt to visit them all.

Here there is evidence of solid training in churchmanship. This morning there was a big group for confirmation, mostly illiterate but full of life. They really seemed to know what they were doing, and the service was reverent and happy. Unfortunately the elders of the congregation spoiled the effect at the reception afterwards. The old hereditary beggar mentality does not die easily and 'The Mission' is still often treated as a sponge to be squeezed. This time the demand is for a bell. It must be admitted that they have built a lovely little church entirely with the money subscribed by their relatives over in the Ceylon tea estates. It is a joy to see it in the midst of the appalling squalor of the leather workers' quarter of the village. But they have so shockingly neglected the school building that, as the Council Chairman remarked, it would probably fall down at the first stroke of the bell. It was this remark which precipitated the unruly ending of the reception. I was able to walk out unnoticed in the middle of the ensuing argument about the relative values of a bell and a school. Probably the argument is still going on. The next congregation to be visited is one of only five families. They have a little prayer house typical of what may be seen in dozens of villages—about ten feet by sixteen feet, mud walls six feet high, thatch roof of bamboo, palmyra leaves, and straw, one window on each side, and a clear, smooth floor of hard mud, washed and disinfected with cow-dung. The altar is of the same hard-baked mud, and it has an altar-cloth embroidered by the girls in the boarding school and a good brass cross. Very quietly and reverently they gather and take part in the brief service. They are new converts and are still at the stage where the prayers are said phrase by phrase to be repeated by the congregation. They will be ready for the first confirmations soon. Two more families have been enrolled as catechumens. There is no resident worker, and a teacher has to come from a village three miles away to take the services. We must open a school here if possible.

Perhaps the most important part of the visitation is the meeting of the Pastorate Committee at the end. A very detailed questionnaire has been sent beforehand to prepare the ground. It covers every aspect of the life of the pastorate: provision of the Word and Sacraments to every village, training in worship, training of workers, distribution of scriptures, hymn books, prayer-books, preparation for confirmation, catechumenate, youth work, evangelistic work, schools and school attendance, family life, marriage problems, church discipline, work among women, training in giving, church organization, maintenance of records, buildings and properties. The presbyter has prepared material for an answer under each head. My two days' touring in the pastorate has given me an idea of the strong and weak points, and I have a page of notes. We sit round a table in the old school building at pastorate headquarters. The oil lamp throws an uncertain light on the group of six men and one woman gathered round it along with the presbyter, the council chairman and myself. The secretary is Isaac, the old catechist, dressed in the long coat that is now out of fashion, with the cuffs long worn to rags. He knows church procedure well, and though he is too busy writing minutes to say much, he finds time to correct us where we go off the proper track. Beyond him sits old Devasaghayam from Gundukulam. He has worked all his life as a labourer and finds no need for a shirt now in his old age. His strong, broad chest has grey hair on it now, and his eyes are failing, but he can speak with force and authority. His second boy has been in the ministry for three years now, and that has helped him to look at church business from a new angle. On his right is Dr. Peter, the doctor in the Government hospital. He has been elected to the committee in deference to his position, but he is a less valuable member than he thinks, being incapable of comprehending any ways of working other than those of the Government. Most of the members are reluctant to disagree with him, and it will not be easy for him to learn. On the bench at my left are Jeevanandam, a retired Revenue Inspector, Vethamuthu, a farmer from the village we visited this morning, and David, a young teacher from the church school at Attapathur. Jeevanandam, who was a convert from one of the criminal tribes, is in a state of uncertain equilibrium between nature and grace, and has to be handled carefully. Vethamuthu is obviously respected by the others as a man of balanced judgment and common sense. I am not sure how far he would follow a really sacrificial Christian lead, but he would be solidly loyal as far as he went. David is obviously a lad to keep an eye on. The pastor tells me that he spent a year in the Ashram at S. before he came into diocesan service. He is dressed with extreme simplicity, and there is a fire in his eye that burns dangerously when the cumbersome machinery of church life seems to impede progress. Now I understand why there are catechumens in his village. I must see him after this meeting. In a chair slightly apart sits old Mrs. Kirubamani, who has worked as a Biblewoman ever since her husband died thirty years ago. She only speaks when she is appealed to. I wish she would speak more. I remember the group of girls she brought for confirmation last year, and the talk I had with her afterwards in her house where the whole of her furniture, apart from cooking-pots, was one rush mat which she asked me to sit on. Hers is the face of one 'far ben' in the counsels of God.

The meeting lasts till nearly ten o'clock. I hope some at least of the decisions will be carried out. I have another two pages of notes for reflection and action at the next opportunity. At last we come to a close with prayer and the benediction, and then sit down happily to a meal of rice and curry.

Afterwards there is a confabulation among some of the members, and Devasaghayam, Vethamuthu and the Doctor advance upon me with all the air of a deputation. I am firmly shepherded into a corner, and with much clearing of throats the matter is explained by old Devasaghayam. When the bishop pays his next visit, will he please come properly dressed? Coming from a man with no shirt, this might call for explanation. Through a cloud of confused Tamil I grasp the fact that a rochet will not do: a cope and mitre are expected—otherwise Romans and others will not hold us in proper respect. A bishop should at least attempt to be magnificent. It is past ten-thirty. This might be a long and complimented argument. I fall back on the easy explanation. 'It is not my custom.' Perhaps that is the lazy way out, but it works. And there are a lot of more important matters to be talked out before bed.

The morning is fresh and lovely, and we are on the road early, headed for P., where there is to be a conference of the High School teachers and a difficult committee about hospital affairs. But that is still two hours away, and meanwhile the day is still cool, the dew lies glistening on the grass and the sun is bright enough to bring out all the rich varieties of colour in trees and tanks and paddy fields, but not yet scorching and terrible as it will be later. The fields are of all shades from the brilliant emerald green of the young seedlings to the gold of the ripe crop, for growth here depends upon what is available in the irrigation tank and not upon what falls directly over the fields. A wayside pool beside a water-channel is almost covered by a rich purple carpet of water-jasmine, and here and there on the earth-bunds between the paddy fields there is a splash of yellow thorn. As we pass the well twenty women are gathered there, drawing their water or waiting their turn, and talking all the time at the pitch of their voices. The brilliantly polished brass pots, each holding about three gallons, are placed on the ground to be filled from the smaller vessels which are used for drawing. There is a steady procession of women carrying their pots home from the well, one on the head and one on the hip, walking with perfect grace of carriage along the narrow path between the paddy fields. A little farther out from the village the cattle boys are driving their slow charges towards the jungle in search of pasture. Soon the tinkle of their bells dies away, and we are out on an open *maidan* where the car speeds ahead over the dry ground, and the tower of the temple at V. is just visible through the clump of trees on the horizon. Two miles beyond V. the road crosses for a short distance the boundary of another pastorate, formerly of the American Mission. Under a wayside tree a small crowd is gathered, and they signal us to stop. Their leader comes forward with a garland: 'Our church is just two furlongs away over the fields. We heard that you were passing this way. Please come and say a prayer in our church.' Neither of my companions had known that there was a congregation here: the old mission boundaries were not often crossed. The meeting has all the flavour of the unexpected. As we walk across the fields I question the group. Their congregation consists of six families of the leather workers' community. They have never had any school or any paid mission teacher. Their leader, Inbanathan, is one of the volunteers who has just finished a month's course at the theological seminary. He has just enough education to be able to read the Bible and conduct a service, and he finds time in the midst of his duties to look after this little flock. Now we have reached the church, which is a very small shed of mud and thatch. Inbanathan marshals his little company before the door to greet me. His face positively glows with pleasure as he does the honours on behalf of the congregation. Then we all go in for a brief prayer. The building is swept spotlessly clean, and there is a fine bowl of flowers on the Table. We all kneel together for prayer, and then I give them the blessing. Then across the fields to the car to hurry on for our Committee.

This is the kind of thing that convinces me beyond doubt that the Church has taken root. I suppose that much of our more impressive work could be easily swept away. These handsome buildings of ours, these magnificent colleges and schools and hospitals which rightly win the praise of the world—they could well be swept away by the hurricanes that are blowing in

Asia and the world. But I do not think what I saw this morning could be blown away: it is too close to the ground. Of course it is still tender. It needs to grow. But I am sure it will hold.

The training and strengthening of these volunteer workers is one of our most pressing duties. In the old days the real pastoral care of the thousands of village congregations was in the hands of the grant-aided teacher-catechist. Selected and trained by the Church, but mainly paid by the Government, he was the real infantryman of the Church Militant here in South India. Week after week, in thousands of villages, he ran the school, the church, the Sunday School, the Young People's class, and whatever else there was, preached the Word in the church and in the street and from house to house, ruled his flock, withstood the contumacious, encouraged the weak, corrected the erring, and continued to be the friend and helper of the whole village —and all on a salary that was just enough to keep him above starvation. Thank God there are still thousands of these men and women carrying on the tradition. But the situation is changing rapidly. Government policies more and more demand the centralization of work in a smaller number of better schools; there is less and less freedom for the teacher to do church work; more and more new congregations have no Christian school to serve them. The training of volunteers is therefore of crucial importance. We have over one hundred and fifty congregations now in charge of volunteer farmers, coolies, Government teachers, officials and others. They are being slowly built up into a corps of trained and consecrated workers, and even though many of them are unlettered and simple men like Inbanathan, I am confident that they hold, in large part, the key to the future of the village churches.

## FOURTEEN

THIS morning's service was a severe trial. When we have so much to learn from each other it is a pity that we should start by learning the wrong things. Of all the glorious riches of the Anglican tradition, why should we begin by borrowing processions and surplices? And why should we be hastening to place the Holy Table against the wall and use it as a shelf for ornaments just when even the Romans are bringing it into the centre of the church and calling on the whole congregation to remember that they are a holy people? In many ex-Congregational churches the old red plush sofa is now inconspicuously tucked away in a corner or cast out into some out-house, and personally I do not shed any tears for it. But the rash of railings which breaks out everywhere distresses me. The trouble is that where Anglicans have had a clear, strong, steady tradition in these matters, the others have often had none. One is inclined to laugh at the incongruity of the word-for-word translation into Tamil of every sentence of the English Prayer Book, and at the incomprehensible cacophonies produced by little Tamil choir boys trying to squeeze long Tamil phrases into the mould of English prose-chanting. But the missions of the Congregational and Presbyterian tradition, at least the Anglo-Saxon ones, have given far too little guidance in liturgical matters. A rigid framework may perhaps be the best thing to preserve life in its early stage. Moreover it is one of the tragedies of the situation that the Churches which have given their ministers the maximum liberty of liturgical improvisations are those which have given them the minimum training in liturgical principles. It is not surprising that a reaction sets in, and people look round for something stable and orderly. But imitation without any understanding of the principles involved is no solution. It will be a poor result of union if we all become imitation Anglicans. We are called to real liturgical reform. The clash of differing traditions ought to compel us to dig deep and lay solid foundations on the real theological principles underlying worship.

Sometimes the clash has been painful. When we meet on diocesan occasions, for councils, committees and retreats, the question has to be settled each time, 'what form of celebration shall we use?' There are often some who find it difficult to share in the unfamiliar form. There is a sound conservatism which I pray to be preserved from breaking. Yet our traditions cannot be the last word. I believe these pains are going to be real means of grace. These are the times when it is good to remember that we did not unite because we wanted to, but because we believed it was the plainly revealed will of our Lord.

We have united on a basis of comprehension. Each

congregation has the right to keep its ways of worship. But comprehension is only the first word and not the last. We begin by accepting each other and forgiving each other as we are. But then the process which is the real meaning of reunion only begins. It is the process of reformation in the light of God's Word and as led by His Spirit; the process of discovering what elements in the comprehensive union are worthy of God's grace and what are not; the process of learning *together* to bring all our varied practices to the test of conformity with the Gospel. That is a process which involves pain. There is no place where it is more painful than in regard to worship. The real meaning of reunion will only be apparent as that process goes on.

One of the questions I had to answer at my consecration was this: 'Will you diligently acquaint yourself with the various forms and methods of worship used in your diocese, and so advise the ministers and congregations committed to your charge that this Church may offer such worship as will be worthy of God's majesty and love, and a witness to those around them?'

Some of the worship offered in the churches does not meet that test. Some things have been changed. There is a deep consciousness that reform is needed, and a deep desire for forms of worship that we can all share together. The meeting of the Liturgical Committees of the Synod and of the Diocese during recent weeks have been a real joy. Nothing so far has done so much to open up real communication between our traditions. We have constantly discovered that our varieties of practice hide identity of belief and desire.

The new liturgy which the Synod is being asked to approve will truly be an expression of much wrestling in the whole Church for the offering of a worship more worthy of God's glory. When we have that in our hands it will be far easier to correct abuses and strengthen sound traditions of worship. We have been able to agree wonderfully quickly about the services of Holy Communion and Confirmation. I think that when we come to deal with the Baptismal services we shall be up against harder and still more fruitful differences.

## FIFTEEN

Last night when I was camping at P., a boy came in from M. with the news that the newly baptized Christians there were suffering terribly from hunger as a result of boycott by their Hindu landlords. We sent off a messenger by the night train with instructions to bring some powdered milk from the hospital and any other supplies available from the gifts received from the American Churches. This morning he returned with half a dozen big tins of powdered milk, and five of us are off on the road north.

On the way our talk is about the struggle in which this is a small incident. There is a mass movement among the leather workers' community in this area, and hundreds have either been baptized or placed under instruction for baptism. They belong to the lowest social stratum of the villages, and their conversion has been bitterly resented by the Hindu landowners. It is very hard for the beneficiaries of an ancient social system to endure such revolutionary changes. 'They that have turned the world upside down have come here also.' These converted leather workers, forsooth, talk about having a school, consort with people much above their station, and altogether behave as if they thought they were God's own children. Moreover, and this is the worst offence, they refuse any longer to smear their foreheads with the sacred ash of Siva when they are sent out to do the drumming for a festival. One of the landlords, a generous-hearted man, has tried to uphold their right to become Christians, but he has been overruled. The rest have determined to crush this revolution. The Christians have been denied access to wells, and have been refused their customary employment. In order to break their resistance, the unprecedented step has been taken of bringing from another village a whole group of Hindu leather workers with their families, and settling them in the village to do the work formerly done by the local leather workers. They have been crushed lower and lower by hunger and despair. Dire threats have been issued as to what will happen if they do not renounce their Christianity by a certain day—a day which is always postponed when it is seen that there is no weakening.

At one moment there was a very serious weakening. Fourteen of the Christian men, driven to dull despair by hunger and unemployment, decided to submit. 'What is the good of it? What's the good of all this misery for the sake of a little bit of ash.

Come on, we'll go and put it on.' They went in a body to the Hindu temple, telling the priest of their intention. Two crowds were watching. On one side, between the temple and the outcaste quarters, the Christians who had learned of the defection stood at a distance and watched. On the other side stood the Hindus. The fourteen men stood in a line in front of the temple. The priest went into the dark inner chamber of the temple and came out with the sacred ash to be given to each man. But something had happened in those men's minds. Instead of holding out their hands to receive it, they simply stood with arms folded. In the stupor of hunger and despair they had agreed to do this thing, but when it came to the moment, they could not deny their Christ. There was a moment of silence, while they stood on the very brink of apostasy. Then one after another spoke: 'Do what you will; we cannot do this.' Together they turned and walked back towards their fellow Christians. In a moment they were joined by their brethren, and the whole company marched back to the squalid slum which was Christ's outpost in that village, and the priest of Kali stood alone before the temple with the sacred ash still in his hand.

That deed sent an electric shock through all the villages in the area. The attempts which were being made in other villages to force the Christians to renounce their faith stopped abruptly. Any tendency among the Christians to weaken disappeared then and there. Henceforth there will be no question of returning to Hinduism. But there is a long, hard road still to travel.

Persecution is no less bitter, and the long-continued famine in the whole area makes everything harder than it would in any case be.

At the village everything seems quiet. We go at once to the leather workers' quarters. It is the most shockingly congested slum I have ever seen. There are about twenty-five small, one-room mud huts, generally having three families in a hut. There is hardly space to walk between the huts. All attempts to get fresh house sites have so far been blocked by the influence of the caste people.

The whole group gathers in a small open space in the centre of the quarter. As I watch them I feel ashamed that we have done practically nothing to help them. Economically they are worse off since they became Christians. They have no school and we have been unable to start one. We have not even been able to place a worker in their midst because there is literally no space to put up a hut for him. I hope that we shall soon succeed in getting the house sites. When that happens doubtless the cry 'rice Christians' will be raised. At the moment they are dull and listless from want of food. The full-cream milk from the tins is now being handed round, and there is sufficient stock to keep at least the children from starvation for some time. But milk does not ease the pangs of an empty stomach. The plans for locating a full-time rural worker in this area must be pushed forward at all costs. He will show them how to get Government land for cultivation, how to use their ancient skill as leather workers to better advantage, and how to run a co-operative society for marketing their products.

Meanwhile what have we given them? We have given them the Gospel. At the moment they don't look much like the Apostles on the day of Pentecost. But these men and women have judged that it is better to suffer starvation and persecution than to give up the Christ of whom they yet know so very little. The older folks don't feel like singing, but the children, with the resilience of their age, are now joining in one of the simple *kummi* tunes, clapping their hands to keep the time, taking up each line after the leader.

*There is one true God who made the whole world.*
*He is the only God, there is none like Him,*
*And He is the Father of us all.*
*All the world is His dear family;*
*He is the dear Father,*
*And so we are all brothers and sisters.*

*Like a shepherd seeking a lost sheep,*
*Like a woman seeking a lost coin,*
*And more lovingly than either*
*He has sought us and found us and made us His children. . . . . .*

This is the foundation on which anything else worth doing will have to be built. This is what has frightened the caste people, because this must in the end mean a revolution.

In this whole area there are more enquirers than we can deal with. It is the sort of situation into which all our concentrated resources ought to be poured, not so much in money as in truly consecrated workers who will live among these people and show them what kind of life the Gospel produces.

It is a joy to pass on to the next village where the new converts have been longer rooted in the Faith and are beginning to bring forth a steady harvest. It is already dark when we get there, and there is hardly room for everyone in the little prayer house. Every family brings an offering of grain or fruit as well as money, and offers it before the service begins. The confirmation takes a long time, for there is a very large group to confirm and much teaching to be done.

Next morning we move to A. Here there is to be the very first confirmation ever held, as the first Christians here were only baptized last year. They are a minority in the village, but it is very clear that others are deeply interested in the Gospel. As I sit with the candidates for an hour and a half testing their understanding of the Faith, the Hindus are standing all around listening with concentrated attention. We have not yet been able to build a church here, and the service takes place in a temporary *pandal.* The confirmation is followed immediately by the first communion. I find it almost inexpressibly thrilling to spread the Lord's Table in a place where it has never been spread before, and to receive for the very first time the fruits of a new village for Christ. One's mind runs forward to the days when, if God wills, a noble church shall stand here, and the Gospel shall have put down deep roots and shall bring forth fruit by holy lives, and the whole village shall be transformed and sanctified by the love of Christ.

## SIXTEEN

THE farther east we go in this diocese, the fewer are the roads. Last night as we ploughed through deep, sandy tracks, and lurched over deep channels and high embankments, I made a firm resolve never to bring the car here again. Once we were completely stuck, and had to get about twenty men to pull the car out of the deep sand. The last part of the journey was in the dark, and we constantly had to send a man ahead with a lantern to find out where 'the road' had gone to. Eventually we reached the village at 9 p.m., and had to begin the confirmation at ten o'clock. This morning I was assured that the road would be quite easy, but was sceptical enough to insist upon taking a crowbar and a couple of digging mattocks. For the last hour we have been using them steadily to clear a track for the car through the jungle. Resting now for five minutes we have ample opportunity to survey the situation in all its absurdity. The heat shimmers off the polished surface of the car, and its gleaming chromium-plating looks completely foolish in the midst of the surrounding cactus and scrub. Away on the horizon there is a faint haze, cloaking the seashore which is our destination. The foreground seems to be full of murderous spikes of cactus plants, each well able and willing to penetrate even the heavy tyres of a modern car. One only learns by experience which of the 'roads' are suitable for cars.

It is after five o'clock when we finally get clear of the jungle. There is a wide sweep of sandy beach ahead, and the car responds with enthusiasm to the improved conditions. In a few minutes we have reached the edge of the little seaside village where we should have been five hours ago. Hope deferred has failed to make the heart sick, for the whole congregation seems to be waiting for us, and our arrival is celebrated with a deafening outburst of drums, fireworks, cheers and music. After the usual garlandings and greetings, we set off together to the little prayer house which they have just built. This large group of about twenty-five families were enrolled as catechumens nearly a year ago. They live largely by bringing firewood over in their little catamarans from the nearby islands to the mainland. As they have to be away for long periods in their boats, their preparation for baptism has been difficult. But there is certainly no doubt about their enthusiasm.

After the reception in the village we set off singing for the nearby lake. It is dark now, and we have to light oil lamps and try to shield them from the wind. The same wind makes it impossible for us to go to the seashore for the baptism, as the waves will be too big. At the lakeside the whole congregation of about two hundred forms a semicircle facing the water, and the first part of the service is conducted from the centre of the semicircle at the water's edge. Then the two presbyters and I wade out till we stand in two feet of water. As the head of each family is called, the whole family comes out together, and then each individual is immersed and signed with the Cross, and returns to the bank to dry and put on spotless clothes. After nearly two hours the baptism is complete. The moon is now high in the sky, and the quiet waters of the lake are turned to silver. The brief conclusion of the service follows, and we all march slowly back to the village. The babies are asleep. For some of the little boys it has been rather a game—this moonlight bathe in the village lake. For many of the adults it has been a deeply meaningful experience. But what matters is that the whole community, men, women and children, has come under the covenant of Christ. Just in front of me a woman trudges along in silence, her baby fast asleep on her hip. Ahead of her is her husband, with an older boy on his shoulder. I saw his eyes when he came to be baptized. Now he walks alone, thinking long thoughts about the day's deed. The boy is pulling his hair and singing a cheerful ditty. 'As many of you as were baptized into Christ did put on Christ.' How dreadful it would have been to leave the children out! Perhaps that baby in front is the wisest of us all.

Early in the morning everyone is crammed into the little prayer house. The glow of their baptism is upon them. No cathedral was ever more glorious. And how easily and swiftly the Apostle's words strike right home to every heart! 'We were buried through Him in baptism.' That is just it! We were dead and buried. (How thankful I am that we were able to give them the full act of immersion.) 'That like as Christ was raised from the dead, so we might walk in newness of life.' The resurrection life begins here now. Thanks be to God for His unspeakable gift.

# SEVENTEEN

ALL morning we have been deafened by the strident Communist demonstrators. They march in procession round the compound shouting slogans until their leaders are almost incapable of articulate speech, and only inarticulate animal noises come out of their sadly overworked throats.

The situation has been steadily deteriorating for some weeks. It has now come to a head over the demand for the abolition of selection examinations. Evidently the whole thing has been carefully organized from outside. The Communists have suffered several defeats in industrial strikes, and are therefore turning their attention to the student front.

It is a very promising front from their point of view. The best minds in the university world have realized for some time that matters were reaching a point where disaster was to be expected. The struggle to obtain university degrees has more and more ceased to have even a nodding acquaintance with any interest in education. It has become more and more simply a matter of economic necessity or ambition. Corruption, the 'leakage' of examination questions, and the reduction of teaching to a process of cramming guided by some system for 'spotting' probable questions have become more and more the regular staple of college life. Those who have some understanding of what a university properly is, have a harder and harder battle.

This is the kind of situation where Communism knows exactly how to manoeuvre. The building up of 'student unity,' the fomenting of strikes on particular issues, and the application of the tactics of class warfare to the relations of students and teachers are all obvious and simple steps for them. Christians, and others who realize that drastic reform is needed, constantly find themselves outmanoeuvred and are helpless when the moment for action arrives. The Communists on the other hand have able workers giving their whole time to 'the student front.' It is not surprising that there has been a wave of student strikes all over India.

Yesterday evening things came to a climax when the students barricaded members of the Faculty in their room and stated that they would not allow them to leave until the students' demands were met. To-day the police have taken charge. They have used tear gas to disperse the mob which is surrounding the Faculty room. Students are scattering wildly and trying to help each other to recover from the effects of the gas. They are using stones now, and smashing all accessible glass. One of the senior professors has been hit, but fortunately not seriously hurt.

The police are loading their guns now and facing the mob of students with stones. They realize that the police are prepared to fire. Their morale cracks and the crowd begins to disappear.

The actual battle is settled. But how long will it take to heal these wounds, to restore to health a community in which spiritual decay has gone so far? That is a challenge indeed. Healing will not come easily. It will need more devotion and skill than we have so far produced. But I am sure they are available.

## EIGHTEEN

For the first time I am making a pastoral tour on the pillion of a motor cycle. My companion is a young American missionary who is in charge of the pastorate. He is expert at weaving his way among the livestock of the country roads, and before long I begin to feel quite comfortable. In my rucksack I have Bible, lyric and prayer-books, Communion vessels, pastoral staff, a change of clothes, and some food and water. Our destination is a small village far up in the hills, and the journey promises to be interesting. It is one of the very few villages left inhabited by still independent representatives of the Puliyan caste which formerly peopled these hills. About thirteen years ago nearly all the villagers became Christians, and a school was started. But it was hard for any teachers from the plains to stay there. It was ten miles from the nearest point to which a wheeled vehicle could be brought, and very malarial. After some years the school had to be closed. Visits from outside became less and less frequent. When I first heard about the village eighteen months ago, it had not been visited for several years. I at once asked that it should be visited, and as a result of this contact was re-established and regular visits were resumed. The villagers were reported to be still loyal to their confession, though terribly ignorant (naturally) of what it involved. One of the young men was brought down for a brief course of training as a volunteer, and a few days ago he returned. I have long wanted to visit the place, and this seems a good opportunity to do so, and to install the young man in his office. There are also some adult baptisms to be administered. The story is an unusual one. During the long period of isolation, the Christian villagers had to face a difficult problem. They are the only Puliyan Christians. The other Puliyan families from whom they would normally expect to get wives for their sons refused to give their daughters unless the Christians renounced their new faith. The latter, in spite of the fact that the Church had treated them with such shocking indifference, absolutely refused to do so. I understand that the problem was finally solved by the ancient method of marriage by capture, and that is why there are candidates for baptism. The situation obviously calls for personal investigation. Meanwhile a catechist has been preparing the girls for baptism.

We have to climb about four thousand feet to the village, and are not sure of the way, but are determined to make the motor cycle go as far as it will. The sun is getting hot by the time we get to the foot of the *ghat*. A road has been built for some distance into the hills to carry down the fruit and other products of the hill estates. For the first few miles it zigzags up the face of a steep hill, thinly covered by thorn. The road is more like a dry torrent bed than a road. Ruts have been worn out by the flood water into rocky channels up to two feet in depth, and boulders worthy of a glacial moraine provide additional variety. After the first half-mile I begin to learn the art of dropping off the back when required, pushing the machine, and then jumping on again. My admiration for the manufacturer of the motor cycle becomes greater with every hazard successfully negotiated.

A small stone go-down by the roadside, built for storing the produce of the estates ready to be sent down to the plains, provides a good place to leave the motor cycle, and we continue on foot. After a mile or two we are met by a group of four of the villagers, sent down to meet us and show us the way. They are a tremendously cheerful, jolly group, full of conversation. We examine with much interest their catapults which they use for getting birds and other small game. After another mile we wade through a deep and swiftly flowing river, and then begin a long climb of about six miles through magnificent forests of vast trees whose names I do not know, with occasional glimpses of range upon range of forest-clad hills stretching away to the west. The paths are only narrow tracks through the forests, and without our guides we should be completely lost in a few minutes. By about two o'clock we have come out on to somewhat less steep slopes, and there are wide areas covered with banana, orange, and cardamom plantations.

Suddenly we come to the edge of a clearing, and the village is below us. It seems to be almost enclosed in a small valley, the floor of which has been skilfully terraced into a series of tiny, irregular-shaped paddy fields, irrigated by a small stream. At the entrance to the village is the church, a fairly solid building with a roof of zinc-sheet well anchored down to withstand storms. In a few moments we are all gathered at the church door for greetings and conversation, and then we all go inside for a more thorough talk. In the course of a long session with them I learn something of their experiences, of the tenacity with which they have clung to their faith in spite of total neglect, and of the efforts they have made to keep in touch with other Christians in the plains. I ask them to say as much as they can remember of the Lord's Prayer, the Creed and the more familiar lyrics. It is clear that a little steady teaching would bring them all back to their memory quite easily.

I gently raise the question of the marriage difficulties. They repeat substantially the story which I had heard. The catechist brings forward four girls whom he has been preparing for baptism—a most cheerful and contented looking group, I must say. 'We stole them,' says one of the men, with disarming simplicity. 'Did they steal any of yours?' I ask. The idea is repudiated with indignation. The catechist, who is naturally feeling a little at sea in this unusual situation, and who remembers some of my recent pastoral letters on the subject of marriage laws, asks, 'What are we to do about calling the banns?' With as much firmness as possible I tell them that I am glad they are so loyal to the Faith, but that stealing brides is wrong, and that in future it must never happen; that, in future, marriages must only be conducted in the Christian way; that I am willing to baptize the four girls if they are ready to accept Christ as their Lord, and to have the marriage regularized. They all promise to abide by the laws of the Church. A short talk with the four girls convinces me that they ought to be baptized, and it is agreed that the service should take place after about an hour.

During the interval we visit all the houses and learn as much as we can of their life, of their triumphs and difficulties. At about five o'clock we gather again for a long and very full service of worship. In this situation we can take very little for granted, and the most thorough preparation and explanation must precede and accompany each act of the service. Yet it would be plainly wrong to give these people less than the fullest that the means of grace given to us can offer. The baptism, the installation of the young man as volunteer in charge (for the time being), and the administration of Holy Communion to those who are communicant members of the Church, all form part of the service, which lasts over three hours. But there is no flagging of attention or reverence. It will take a long time to undo all the effects of this long neglect, but there can be no doubt whatever that the foundations stand firm and ready for rebuilding.

Next morning we have to leave at four o'clock to be down at the foot of the hills for my next engagement. For nearly two hours we walk in the pitch darkness through the narrow forest tracks with only the light of a hurricane lantern. As we go, we talk of these hill people, of the almost total lack of evangelistic work among them, and of plans to find and send up men who will be willing to live among them and serve them for Christ's sake. By the time we reach the motor cycle it is broad daylight, and by nine o'clock we are down on the plains, and the congregation of S. is waiting at the church door. In a few minutes the village in the hills has slipped over the horizon of the mind, and one realizes with a start how terribly easy it is to forget what does not clamour for attention.

## NINETEEN

A MESSAGE has just come that Sundaram, the evangelist at M., died in hospital in the early hours of this morning. This is heavy news to bear. I saw him yesterday, very weak and hardly able to speak, but with the same indomitable courage and cheerfulness as always. The scene of my first meeting with him has been very vividly before my mind in these last days. It was about eighteen months ago, and I was paying my first visit to that part of the diocese. Coming along a rough cart-track in rather sparsely peopled country, I was surprised suddenly at the sight of a very large crowd. At the head of them stood a remarkable figure —attired in very faded battle-dress, immense army boots and a very much battered topee, the military appearance being further enhanced by a magnificent black moustache. In his hand he carried a long polished baton of stainless steel, slung from his wrist by a leather strap. At my approach he executed a flourish with the baton, and the entire crowd performed a simultaneous genuflection. At another signal they rose and advanced with loud beating of drums and blowing of trumpets. The village church was still only partly built, and as Sundaram had collected the Christians from about ten villages round about, it was necessary for the whole proceedings to be in the open air. My discomfort at this semi-military reception was swallowed up in admiration at the way Sundaram marshalled his hosts. After the service I managed to get a few minutes' private talk with him. I found him to be a man of very little education, but of immense faith and courage. He and his wife were looking after the Christians in a large circle of villages, and living on a miserable pittance which a scavenger in Government service would certainly regard as inadequate. I asked him where he got the stainless steel baton, and he told me the following story. When the Japanese invaded Burma he was unable to escape to India and had to remain in the country. He spent a good deal of his time going from house to house among the Tamil people, reading the Bible to them and doing evangelistic work. While he was thus engaged he was reported to the Japanese authorities as a British spy, arrested, and taken to the nearest Japanese military post. There he was searched and all his possessions, including his Tamil Bible, were taken from him, and he himself was bound hand and foot to a post. Some time later a Japanese officer came into the building. Seeing Sundaram's belongings on the table, he began idly to turn them over. The Tamil Bible interested him. He began turning over the pages and examining it closely. Then he looked up at Sundaram with an expression of enquiry, and made the sign of the Cross on the palm of his hand. Sundaram wagged his head in assent. There was a pause. Then the officer went up to Sundaram and stood alongside him, with his arms spread out in the position of crucifixion. Then he cut the ropes with which Sundaram was bound, gave him his Bible and his other possessions, handed to him this steel baton, and sent him away. Since then Sundaram had always kept it with him and used it as a sort of symbol of office. This is the story he told me; I have, of course, no means of verifying it.

Lately he has had constant illness. Whenever I visited him in hospital he always had the same infectious faith and courage, and he communicated it to the patients in the ward with him. Recently he was discharged, and it was thought that he was cured. Now he has gone on ahead. What a joy it will be to see him among the great multitude that no man can number! His face will shine with its true glory then.

After the funeral I have to go and call on Mr. John about his lawsuit. This case has become very difficult. When village people quarrel we generally manage to settle things without very great difficulty—partly because they are too poor to go to law. Some of the village elders, some leading people in neighbouring villages, and the pastor will sit down together, and after four or five hours—probably sometime after midnight—will come to a settlement. This work of settling quarrels is one of the important parts of the Church's work, and I have never been able to understand those who think of it as an interruption. But when influential members of city congregations quarrel, things are more difficult. In this case there have been some very horrible features, and there will have to be excommunications unless things change very radically. The complications have been introduced by the fact that both parties have appealed to the Courts, and then try to argue that—since they have done so—the Church cannot interfere. I am prepared to risk anything rather than submit to this, and have threatened both parties with ecclesiastical discipline if they do not submit their case to the Court of the Diocese, and withdraw their court cases. This will be a test case of some importance for the future.

I believe that the reason why quarrels, and the settling of quarrels, play such a large part in the life of the Church here is that the whole structure of society is such that people are much more fully involved in each of their social relationships than is the case in the Western type of multiple society. In the typical Western city, each individual is involved in an immense number of relationships each of which only engages a very small part of his total personality. It is possible for him to live a very full life without even knowing the name of his next-door neighbour. He can, to a very large extent, choose the relationships in which he will engage and avoid those which he finds difficult. The Church is only one among the great variety of societies in which he can find his relationships. And even the Church offers him a wide variety of different societies among which he can choose the one that suits his taste. The position in an ordinary Indian village or small town is completely different. The whole of a man's life—his work, his recreation and his religion—is lived in relation to the same set of people. Whichever way he turns, he meets the same people. He cannot replace them with others. And even the Church—the one fellowship which stands in the village in the Name of Christ—insists that it is the place where *all* men are to be at home. He cannot choose his company there either. Moreover, in the Church he is involved in a society which insists on including men and women of all castes, and on demanding that the natural motive of the family solidarity shall be subordinated to the interests of the Church as a whole. It is not really surprising that quarrels are frequent and bitter, or that they are generally eventually healed. They are essentially quarrels between people who know that they cannot finally repudiate one another.

In demanding that quarrels should be submitted to 'the saints' and not to the civil courts, one is, of course, committing oneself to almost unlimited obligations. One would be thankful to leave many of these things to a civil court. But it seems one of the plainest teachings of Scripture that we should not do so. Yet we must always have a penitent sense of the dangers involved in making totalitarian claims on behalf of the Church. Church courts are made up of sinful men. It is as one becomes involved in these situations that one becomes vividly aware of the fact that the Church is both holy and sinful and that God is greater and wiser than His Church, and has resources beyond the resources of the Church.

# TWENTY

Down on the east coast palm trees are almost as thick as grass. For miles and miles they stretch along the shores of the Bay of Bengal, millions and millions of them forming a green girdle around the shores of India. To-day, in the bright morning sun, I am out with a group of Christian palmyra climbers to learn something of their art. There is no chance of bringing the car to these parts, and yesterday afternoon we left our bullock cart behind and walked to the little village by the shore. The roar of the surf grew louder and louder as we tramped over the sand through the endless forests of palmyra palm and then suddenly we stood in sight of the ocean—a great shining expanse of glorious and vivid blue. There was an interval between the congregational reception and the evening service, and we slipped down to the beach for a hurried bathe. The moon was full, and as one looked back towards the land from some distance out, the scene was indescribably lovely—the dark curtain of palms stretching away to the horizon on both sides, the long, silvery line of sand below it, and the glittering water all around, broken here and there by the silhouetted figures of a couple of fishermen bringing their catch home late in their frail *catamaran*.

This morning, after an early Communion, we set off to walk to the next village, and a group of church members—men and women and children—is accompanying us as far as their camp out among the trees. For several months of the year they camp out in small temporary huts, while the tapping is in progress. The whole process is a fascinating example of the brilliant adaptation of means to ends which may be achieved by a very simple people who, if they were to perish from the earth, would leave behind nothing except a few knives by which a future archaeologist could identify their 'culture.' As we walk along, Samuel, our guide, shows us how to distinguish the various types of trees, and explains the methods used in tapping. Each man carries a pouch made of local fibre slung from his waist, a small knife and a stock of lime. He has a ring of strong fibre about eighteen inches in diameter and a small mud pot. At the foot of each tree he puts down his pot, slips the ring over his ankles so as to support the pressure of the soles of his feet against the smooth trunk, and in a very few seconds he has climbed up thirty or forty feet to the tuft of the tree. Holding himself on with his feet and one hand, he deftly empties into his pouch the sweet juice which has collected in a small pot slung below the long sheath of the tree. Then he cuts a thin slice off the end of the sheath, replaces the pot, puts a little lime in it to prevent fermentation, puts his knife back into his belt, and in a few seconds is back at the bottom of the tree pouring the juice from the pouch into the mud pot. So proceeding from tree to tree he soon has a pot full of the thick, sweet juice. He carries this over to the hut where his wife has already got three or four big pots of juice boiling over hot fires of palmyra leaves. The boiling goes on for hours until all the water is boiled away, while the impurities have been skimmed off with spoons made of cocoanut shell. Finally the thick syrup is poured out into moulds of cocoanut shell where it hardens into the solid round balls of jaggery which are sold in the bazaar. Apart from the small knife, there is not a single piece of apparatus required for the whole industry which is not produced in the village, nor—with the same exception—would a single trace of it be left for the spade of an archaeologist after a hundred years. The huts, the mud pots, the cocoanut spoons, and the climbers' wallets and belts would all have crumbled into the surrounding dust. Yet here is a Christian civilization, and this family has just knelt with us at the Lord's Table.

As we walk and talk, however, we are concerned with problems of more immediate history. The introduction of prohibition throughout the state has complicated life very much for these people. It has certainly brought immense benefit to the country as a whole. Drink has been a terrible source of evil in the villages, and prohibition has been magnificently successful in cutting out these evils at the source. But, of course, prohibition can only be enforced by means of a very drastic control of the activities of the palmyra climbers in order to see that the sweet juice is not used for making toddy, and this means very abrupt interference with the ancient customs and methods of these simple people. Under the prohibition laws only members of approved co-operative societies under strict Government control may tap the trees, and they may only do so at certain hours under stringent regulations. There is the usual and probably inevitable red tape. Co-operative societies cannot be formed and approved until an immense number of forms have been filled up in triplicate and passed back and forward several times to and from the officers concerned. Sometimes things do not move unless someone undertakes in person the four hundred mile journey to Madras to persuade the clerk concerned to take the form from the bottom of the file and put it on top. It takes a long time for primitive people to learn the tricks of bureaucracy, and meanwhile families starve and many thousands of trees are permanently ruined through being left untapped for months. Now, Samuel tells us, things are getting straightened out, and the necessary permits have been got, but the damage done to the trees cannot be made good for many decades.

The smell of the boiling jaggery is almost suffocating as we gather for a few minutes' prayer in Samuel's little hut. All his family are there, including his eldest girl, who is in the seventh standard at the boarding school. Her tin trunk would probably survive for the archaeologist's spade. No doubt the future is hers. But for the present and for eternity we are all one in Christ Jesus.

## TWENTY-ONE

In the heart of the old town of M., the streets are very narrow, and the houses of the rich merchants present a miserly front to the world. As we walk along in the hot afternoon there is an oppressive feeling in the air. Heavy wooden doors studded with massive spikes guard the entrances to the houses, and in some cases there are also modern steel gates of the type one associates with an electric lift. To get into the houses one has to mount a very steep stone stairway, which spans the open drain down the side of the narrow street.

The pastor stops outside a particularly formidable looking doorway. 'This is Esther's house; she is expecting us,' he says. Esther is one of a large number of women, wives of wealthy Hindu merchants, who have accepted Christ and been baptized secretly. Her husband is a leading man in the town with a big cloth business in Madras and Tuticorin. In the early days of her Christian life she suffered terrible persecution. Those were the days when she had to slip away secretly at night or in the very early morning to meet at church with others in the same position, so that they could pray for one another and for their husbands. Now Esther is more fortunate than others. Her husband's attitude has changed to one of kindly tolerance. Esther is allowed to practise her religion openly, to give generously to the Church, and to bring up her daughters (but not her sons) as believers. But all attempts to press upon her husband the claim of Christ are met with good-humoured ridicule. I have often asked why these men, who are daily witnesses of the radiant Christianity of their wives, do not themselves become Christians. The answer has always been the same: 'We understand enough of the principles of Christianity to know that it would involve a complete change in our business practices. We cannot afford it.'

Esther has invited us round to meet her husband, and here he is standing at the top of the steps to welcome us. We are at once welcomed into a small room furnished with chairs in European style. Ornate pictures of Hindu gods, and scenes from Hindu mythology are hung all round the room. Esther comes forward with hands clasped in greeting. In a few moments we are seated on chairs. The womenfolk sit on the floor—two of Esther's daughters, one of her Christian friends from a neighbouring house, and Sarah the Bible-woman. Sarah is one of those people who will surely be very great in the Kingdom of Heaven. She is the kind of worker who puts to shame our big institutions, our modern publicity methods, our complicated organizations. Armed with nothing except the whole armour of God, she goes quietly from house to house, working all the time in an atmosphere heavy with all the evil of paganism, and bringing the power of the Gospel to these women, so that they are enabled to live Christian lives right in the heart of Hinduism. Every time I meet her, and those like her, of whom, thank God, there are many, in wealthy Hindu homes as well as in squalid, outcaste villages, I feel that the whole of our ecclesiastical and missionary organization is being challenged. We have created for ourselves unlimited 'points of contact'; have we used them?

Esther is back again with a tray of fruit and cool drinks in graceful silver cups. Her husband disappears into another room and adjusts the radio so that the music becomes a quiet background for conversation.

His youngest daughter comes forward with a small fan to offer some relief from the oppressive heat. One marvels again at the wonderful grace of Indian hospitality. Both husband and wife want to wait on us, but we persuade them to sit down. Esther says laughingly, 'You must talk to my husband; he's terribly obstinate. I have told him so much about Jesus, but he will not listen.' Veerabuttran smiles and looks at me. 'Why do you not accept Christ as your Saviour?' I ask. 'You have seen what He has done for your wife. You have read His words and His deeds. Is there any to compare with Him? Why do you reject Him?' 'I don't reject Him. On the contrary, I admire Him very much. But why should I not admire others also? Why Jesus only?' I open the Bible and read to him. 'Thomas said unto Him, Lord, we know not whither thou goest; and how can we know the way? Jesus saith unto him, I am the way, the truth and the life; no man cometh unto the Father but by me.' There is silence. I can see that Esther and Sarah are praying. 'Don't you see that the Man who said things like that forces you to a decision? If this claim was true, then, of course, you must accept it; if it was false, then the man who made it was a rank imposter, and you ought not to admire him at all. He will not leave you to be a mere admirer.' Veerabuttran shakes his head. 'No, everything is of God, and God is One. Never mind what name you call Him. There's good in every way, and I am not going to change.' Esther laughs again. 'It's no use, man's words cannot do it; the Holy Spirit must do it. That is what I am praying for, and I know He will do it.' Veerabuttran laughs good-humouredly. 'Well, we shall see,' he says. The radio has switched over to a news bulletin, and he goes out to turn it off. Esther wants us to have Bible reading and prayers. As I am reading, Veerabuttran comes back and sits down, listening intently. When we kneel for prayer he gets up to go out, then stops in the doorway and stands there till the prayer is finished —undecided.

Late at night, long after the ordinary service is over, a small congregation gathers in the church. At least it seems very small in the still spaciousness of the great darkened church, but if one counts it there must be sixty women and a good group of men. The occasion is the baptism of two believers for whom it is not yet possible to have baptism publicly. They are both young women married to merchants in the town. They have counted the cost and are prepared to pay it. The familiar words have a very special force spoken at that quiet hour, and in the midst of a group of Christians who have known what it is to suffer for the faith: 'We receive this person into the congregation of Christ's flock, and do sign her with the sign of the Cross, in token that hereafter she shall not be ashamed to confess the faith of Christ crucified, and manfully to fight under His banner against sin, the world, and the devil; and to continue Christ's faithful soldier and servant until her life's end.'

After the service is over a little group of women goes with each of the newly baptized women to her home. As I watch them go off through the quiet streets to face the inevitable hard and lonely battle, my thoughts crystallize into a prayer that God may raise up men to occupy the bridgehead which these brave women have won at so much cost.

## TWENTY-TWO

THE struggle between the Communists and the police has been growing in intensity, and I have only slowly begun to understand the way in which it would bear on the Church. A very large number of our members are workers in the mills, and in the complicated struggle between rival labour unions they have for the most part identified themselves with the Union of which the Communists have got control. Very few indeed have the slightest understanding of the issues involved. As usual they are manoeuvred into position by the expert Marxist workers. With the Government decision to ban the Communist party, the Communists have gone underground, but the war has gone on—wholesale arrests on one side, burnings and murders on the other. When war breaks out there is not much discrimination between guilty and innocent. Late last night I was called out by one of the presbyters who sent a message that twenty of his members had been arrested and sent to the lock-up. I went to see them and have a word with them at the police station, but could get no information as to the charges against them. Now a group has just arrived to say that police lorries drove into the

'Paradise Gardens' quarters at one o'clock this morning, and that about forty men, including twelve Christians, were dragged out of their houses, beaten and taken away. It is alleged that one notorious fellow, T., was the informant who guided the police, and that the operating motive was a purely personal one connected with a recent case of immorality in which a member in the other Union was involved. I promise to do what I can both to see the police and also to try to arrange for bail, and set off at once to the police headquarters. The officer-in-charge is naturally reserved. He is not impressed by my choice of friends. 'If you Christians are going to support this kind of thing, where are we going to?' Finally it comes out that some Christians are wanted in connection with a recent brutal murder, and that it is believed that the murderers are being protected.

Heavy of heart I go over to the other side of the city for a talk with the presbyter of the parish concerned. We agree that he should call a meeting of the leading mill workers among his members for eight-thirty tonight. Meanwhile we go over together to 'Paradise Gardens.'

As one would expect from the name, it is the filthiest slum in the city. Several hundred families are crowded together in small hovels in an area surrounded by high buildings and barbed wire. There is only one exit, down a long, narrow street, and I am told that the Communists control that exit when they want to. The lanes between the houses are so narrow that it is difficult for two people to walk abreast down them because of the cattle tied at the doors. The middle of the narrow lane is occupied by an open drain. Flies, stench and filth are everywhere. There was formerly one small mud hut in the centre, used for common social activities, but the police have recently pulled it down as it was stated to be a centre of Communist activity. As we walk along, calling at the Christian homes to sit and talk and pray, many of the women are weeping. Most of the people, compared to an average village group, are well fed, but in some homes they are suffering greatly. Some have been out of work ever since they were dismissed in connection with the strike eighteen months ago, and their families are showing the effects of long undernourishment. Poor B., for whose reinstatement I have pleaded in vain, died just a fortnight ago. He simply crumpled up under an attack of pneumonia, and his widow and six children are left to carry on the fight. I have promised to see that they get help to complete their schooling. Most of the men are away—either at work or in hiding for fear of further arrests. One thing we must do at once is to get that little hut in the centre rebuilt as a centre for vital Christian prayer, witness and help. That can be done and it will have immense symbolic value.

On my way home I call in at the magistrate's court. Fortunately he is free to give me an interview. He is very helpful in guiding my fumbling attempts to learn the ropes in this new kind of problem.

On the verandah a welcome sight awaits me, old Vethanayagam with two dozen fine new baskets of the gayest colours. This village basket industry really has possibilities. Two years ago when I first visited the small Christian village where Vethanayagam lives, I was struck by two things—the deplorable squalor of a village which had been completely Christian for half a century, and the wonderful skill of its people in weaving coloured baskets and boxes from the local palmyra leaf. I found that the amount they earned in the local bazaar by selling their baskets was so small as to make the work hardly worth while. I asked a group of them to go and take a few days' training from the Industrial Superintendent of one of the Diocesan Industrial Schools, so that they could learn improved styles and patterns which could be sold in Madras and other cities. It has been hard work to make any progress, and the superintendent has had to wage an unremitting battle for proper standards in design and workmanship. But evidently Vethanayagam is trying, and I am sure this can become a real means of lifting at least one village out of its squalor.

The post brings news of another development at the other end of the diocese, where the newly appointed Diocesan Rural Worker is trying to start a co-operative tanning society for the newly baptized Christians of the leather workers' community. At first sight the scheme looks alarmingly expensive, but I hope it can be carried through. It should surely be one of the most obvious and elementary ethical fruits of conversion that the believers can develop that stable basis of mutual confidence on which co-operative enterprise has to be built. I am sure that basis is being laid. The same letter from the rural worker brings cheering news about the well in the outcaste quarters at K. For years the villagers have been writing petitions to the Government asking that the well should be deepened. Inspectors have come and gone, but nothing has been done. Every summer the well runs dry. Now the rural worker writes that he has persuaded the villagers to start deepening the well themselves, and that they expect to have it finished in a few days. That is the beginning of a real spiritual revolution.

As I drive through the thronged streets to the meeting with the mill workers, I have to confess that I have no very clear idea of what I am to say, or of what I expect the meeting to achieve. But somehow or other we must clearly get to grips as Christians with this tangled and tragic situation, and seek prayerfully to find out what God has to say to us about it. We gather in a corner of the great empty church. Some of the men are rebellious and bitter. Some are frightened and anxious only for security at any cost. It is the struggle between the two labour unions which is the main issue in their minds, and it has come as a shock to find that they are already entangled in a conflict with much wider and graver implications. I try to help them to see the political meaning of what they are doing in relation to the whole future of India, and then to show how obedience to the Gospel must direct us in a situation like this. Above all I try to show them that the existence of the Church in the midst of this situation is of decisive importance, that here is a place where forgiveness and fellowship and freedom are actually known and experienced as realities, and that therefore we have our own special and unique duty to do in the situation and are not to allow ourselves to be made pawns in anybody else's game. These thoughts strike home because they correspond to experienced realities. We end with some concrete plans about that building in Paradise Gardens.

After the meeting the presbyter and I spend a very blessed half-hour in the Beggars' Home near by. I find that we sometimes see things more clearly from that point of vision than from anywhere else. There is a faithful Christian there, and a work of the Holy Spirit. We have prayer with those who are looking forward to baptism. One is blind, and I believe that he is going to be granted his sight. This is the kind of place where one really understands the power of the Gospel.

## TWENTY-THREE

SITTING this morning on the edge of a great rock, I feel as if I were in a dream world lifted up above the ordinary earth. The waterfall beside me plunges down the cliff for hundreds of feet, and then is lost to view in the thick tangled jungle below. Here and there a gleam of white reveals the course of the torrent as it roars down the jungle-covered slope until it comes out into the open and begins its journey across the brown, sun-baked plain four thousand feet below. Across the wide valley to the west stands the wall of the Western *Ghats*, rising away southward to the tangled mass of hills around the Periyar Lake. Behind me stretch the forest-clad summits of the High Wavys, and the wide, stretching tea gardens which cover their lower slopes. Smoke rises lazily in the warm air where the old forest is being cleared to make room for new planting. In the deep jungle beside us the voice of the innumerable cicadas competes with the roar of the waterfall to fill the still air with sound.

The big tea factory is out of sight now, and the trim white houses and offices around it. Yesterday it was put to a new use when we had a great service in the ground floor, and I preached from a pulpit of tea chests. Hundreds of Christians from villages all over the diocese have found employment here, and it was a joy to be able to meet with them both in the big central service at the factory and also at some of the outlying stations.

For two glorious days I have enjoyed the hospitality of the planters and tasted the thrill of a pioneer settlement among the wild hills. All around the area of cultivation stretch hundreds of square miles of uncharted jungle where there are no tracks but those of the wild elephant, the tiger and the cheeta. To the east lies the great basin of the Varushanad, inhabited only by wild hill tribes who have no villages, no agriculture and no domestic animals, but live as they wander through the jungle by collecting roots and nuts and leaves both for their own use and for sale or barter to the people of the plains. So wild are they that even the coolies on the estate talked to me of them as one would of interesting wild animals. Christian work is going on among them, but I gather that they are being slowly exterminated by the vicious type of malaria which infests the Varushanad. Here is a challenge which must certainly be taken up.

This afternoon I have to go down to the plains again, but this morning it is good to sit and look at them from afar. We have spent the morning in following down the course of this stream. A little farther up there was a lovely pool where I bathed. Now we have come to the edge where it plunges down the cliffs to the plains below. As we sit with our legs dangling over the edge, the villages in the valley below have an unreal dream-like quality. There is N., where the deacon has quarrelled with the congregation and we have to have a *panchayat* to-night and try to settle it. Away to the right is K., where the church roof fell in. When I first went there and saw it I was so grieved that I called all the Christians in the place (there were only four families) to come into the ruined church and pray for its restoration. Only four months later I received the pastor's letter asking me to come and dedicate the restored building. The local Government school teacher had given a month's salary, his wife had pawned her jewels, the pastor's wife had sold her sewing-machine, and even a Hindu clerk in the local Board Office had made a cross to put on the top. It is a pity that we can't see the church from here now. Over there to the west is C., where they had such a fine Christian Home Festival last month. As a result of it there has been a real revival in the church, not only affecting family life, but generally quickening the whole life of the church. Every morning they get up at five o'clock and call all the members to church for prayers before the day begins. Perhaps if we had been here at five o'clock we might have been able to see the bright light which they have recently installed on the tower of the church to remind all men of the worship they owe to God.

But now we cannot see the bustling life of those villages spread out like a map below us. Here everything speaks of a peace and strength that man cannot make and cannot destroy. Surely it was in just such a place as this that the poet stood who wrote the 106th Psalm, turning from all the majesty of nature, from the mysterious life of the wild beasts, with their own dominion in the hills and forests, to man in his littleness and greatness—man who goeth forth to his work and to his labour until the evening. 'O Lord, how manifold are thy works. In wisdom hast thou made them all. The earth is full of thy riches.'